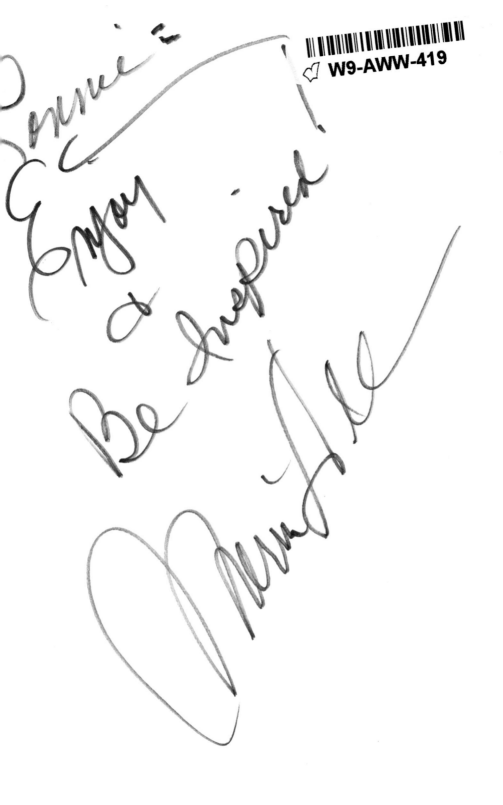

8/14

# Merri Dee

## LIFE LESSONS ON FAITH, FORGIVENESS & GRACE

Life To Legacy, LLC

Merri Dee: Life Lessons on Faith, Forgiveness & Grace
By: Merri Dee

ISBN-10: 1939654017
ISBN-13: 978-1-939654-01-4

Printed in the United States
10 9 8 7 6 5 4 3 2

Cover design: Lewis E. Lee Jr.
Cover photo: Bill Richert Photography
Literary consultation and editing: Clarence Waldron/CW Media
Graphics consultant: Kevin J. Campbell
Publisher: Life To Legacy, LLC
www.Life2Legacy.com
All photographs are courtesy of the author unless otherwise noted.
Books available at MerriDee.com
Amazon.com BarnesandNoble.com

# Contents

# Contents

# Foreword

Merri Dee and I have been sister-friends for more than 40 years. All I want you to know is that I love her. I love her dearly and I cannot envision a time when Merri Dee won't be in my life.

People know Merri Dee as the trailblazing TV and radio icon. She is certainly that. But there is a more personal, girl-next-door side of her that I appreciate. The Merri Dee I know is a great cook who loved to whip up the kind of comfort food that provided a touch of home to road-weary entertainers traveling to Chicago.

In fact, that is how we met. Back in the 1970s, I traveled all across the country and regularly performed at Chicago clubs like Mr. Kelly's and the London House, as well as the Regal and Mill Run theaters. Merri Dee was a radio disc jockey and hosted a TV show that profiled many African-American entertainers. Because entertainers finished work in the wee hours of the morning when most restaurants were closed, it was not uncommon for Merri Dee to invite performers to her home for a meal. After one of my performances, I accepted her invitation. The warmth of her hospitality sparked a friendship that has lasted all these years. I have been blessed by her presence in my life.

I am so pleased that Merri Dee has finally found the time and energy to write this book. More than simply a recitation of her life's journey, this book provides some of her hard-won lessons on how to be victorious in the face of pain and sorrow. Your challenges may not be as dramatic as some of Merri Dee's, but they may feel just as debilitating, just as troubling.

Merri Dee teaches all of us it is not what happens to you that matters most. What is more important is how you respond to what happens. Her life is a living testament of that belief. She has been through so much and has lasted so long. She is simply fabulous. With an unwavering faith in God, she has consistently beaten the odds with style, grace and remarkable courage.

She is such a thoughtful and generous woman. Merri Dee wants everyone to enjoy the best life possible. I am certain she can help you overcome your own challenges, or at least find another way of viewing them. As you read the following pages, cry if you must, laugh where you want, but most of all, think about how you can take Merri Dee's powerful message of hope, faith, resilience and courage to make your own life better.

Much Love!
Nancy Wilson
March 2013

# Acknowledgments

I am so grateful to so many people who encouraged me to write this book. To Toya, my daughter and best-best friend forever, who supported me in my ups and downs. To my darling husband, Nicholas, who has been my rock, a total support system. My granddaughter, Marissa Campbell, who is dreaming her own big dreams; grandsons, Kevin J. Campbell, my graphics consultant, and Jordan Campbell; my son-in-law, Kevin S. Campbell; and my sisters and brothers, Doris, Buster, Alphonse, Thyra and Ernest for loving me.

My deepest appreciation to my many friends who helped shape this book, including my very best friend, the legendary songstylist Nancy Wilson who wrote the foreword; the late Judge Abraham Lincoln Marovitz; the late Drs. Frances Holliday and Melvin Maclin; Val Masters and the late Dr. Bob Masters; Attorney and Pastor Richard Wright and wife, Julia Ann Wright; Danny Markus; the late Teddy Pendergrass; Jann Honore; Stedman Graham; Willie Gault; Jim Brown; Ramsey Lewis; Marilyn McCoo; Billy Davis Jr.; Phil Donahue; MaryJo Basler; Rosemary Matzl; Dolores

Kohl of Kohl Children's Museum; the Roger Salters, father-son duo of Sanmar Financial; my favorite designer, HAJ of HAJ Designs; Dr. Willie Wilson of Omar Medical; my mentors, the late business executives, Sherman Abrams and Carl Silver; Dennis FitzSimons, CEO of McCormick Foundation and loving wife, Ann; Stella Foster; and all my media friends.

I appreciate the commitment of Beverly Price, who sat with me and did the first interviews. Jan Carcerino, who took the interviews, transcribed them and guarded them with her life. Ava Youngblood introduced me to Dawne Simmons of Word Storm Communications who valued my long history of words; Clarence Waldron, adjunct journalism professor, Northwestern University, for his dedicated guidance and editing; and Karen Clay and Celeste Johnson for title creation.

Special thanks to good friend, Andrew Hayes, who always said, "Your story is amazing and must be told." To hair stylist Talona Wilson and makeup artist Earl J. Nicholson for their amazing talents.

I also want to thank all of the believers—colleagues, taxi drivers and others who stopped me on the street through the years and asked, "When are you going to get that book out? It will be so inspiring to so many people."

To all, you have helped me live my life with an attitude of gratitude.

Lovingly,
Merri Dee

# Dedication

This book is dedicated with immeasurable love to Nanny and Pappy—my grandparents, Emily and John Blouin, who believed I would always beat the odds.

# Introduction

When Merri Dee speaks, everyone listens. She has that commanding presence and elegance that make you sit up and pay attention. You want to touch her "lucky hands." When she smiles, you smile with her because you know she is genuine.

I have enjoyed a front row seat in this woman's life. I have watched her grow into the most dynamic woman I know. Who am I? I am her daughter and no one knows better than me that my mother has suffered more than any one woman should. The great part is I have seen her emerge stronger and wiser after each challenge.

You may know her as the woman who had an awesome 43-year broadcasting career—with 38 of those years spent at Chicago's superstation WGN-TV. She was Illinois' first lottery lady, anchored the midday news and sports, hosted a magazine-style TV show and served in management as Director of Community Relations.

If you have known Merri Dee for a long time, you will remember that she was the first African-American to model in the Chicago Auto Show. That's where it all began for her. She was one of the first female disc jockeys on radio where she spun the vinyl on WSDM and opened her four-hour radio show at WBEE with Quincy Jones' hit, "Killer Joe," as "Merri Dee the Honeybee."

You may think you know all about Merri Dee, but you are in for a big surprise. In this book, she shows how she used her "second beginning" (life after she was kidnapped and shot) as a way to help others. She candidly recalls growing up without her mother, who died when she was only 2 years old, and being left in the hands of a physically and verbally abusive stepmother. She left home at 14, married at 19, gave birth to me at 21 and divorced at 28.

People often ask me, "What is Merri Dee really like? Is she always so happy? How can she always be so positive, so strong and so inspirational?" I can honestly tell you that what you see is definitely what you get.

My mother is warm, kind, sensitive, smart, challenging, intuitive and a whole lot of fun. She is engaging and captivating and has a will of steel and a heart of gold. She is a sophisticated, yet down-to-earth woman you would love to call your friend. Merri Dee is always paving the way for others with her belief, "If it is to be, it is up to me."

I'm one of the lucky ones. She has always been the anchor and the rock in my life, guiding me and sharing her wisdom. Now, thanks to her book, "Life Lessons on Faith, Forgiveness & Grace," you too can walk with her as she recalls her sometimes painful, yet triumphant and amazing journey.

Toya Campbell
Best Friend & Daughter

*Introduction*

# Prologue

As I lay face down on the ground, my white silk pantsuit stained black with mud and two .38-caliber bullets lodged in the back of my head, somehow, someway, I realize that I'm not dead. I'm still alive. Kidnapped and left for dead on the side of the Calumet Expressway on the far South Side of Chicago. I'm alive. I'm alive. Yes, I am alive! It was indeed a miracle. A bona fide, authentic, life-defining moment.

But what characterizes this moment, and every moment that has shaped me throughout the decades, has less to do with the event, and more to do with my response, reflected in the simple, yet eloquent lyrics of the late gospel legend Albertina Walker's gospel song, "I'm Still Here."

I think back to the first time I heard Albertina sing that song, my personal anthem of empowerment. I was sitting behind the pulpit in one of Chicago's many South Side churches, listening as the organ boomed the first thunderous chords, followed by Albertina's warm and throaty vocals.

My body shivered as goose bumps rose on my arms. All I could do was wrap my arms around me in a self-embrace. Albertina and I had been friends for years, so I know that she didn't write the song for me, yet in many ways I feel connected to the tune as if I had been there at its birth.

Those lyrics mirror so many events in my life. Growing up a motherless child. Feeling unloved and mistreated. Tormented and tortured. Discarded by a woman who controlled my life. Albertina's vibrant singing told of my guilt and anguish of having a stillborn first child. It expressed my self-reproach for an unfortunate first marriage and my fear and humiliation at being a victim of domestic violence. It lamented my kidnapping and attempted murder.

When I listen to Albertina's signature tune, I recall Roberta Flack's "Killing Me Softly With His Song." Albertina truly was singing my life with her song.

That is the beauty of "I'm Still Here." It proclaims that hard times are not the complete narrative of any life, especially mine. Instead of wallowing in the depths of depression, I choose to view my defining moments as a testament of God's love.

Our lives are filled with transformative moments; some that are so awesomely wonderful that they take our breath away. Others so horrible we may question our ability to continue breathing. What difference would it have made on that fateful day in my life if I had gone straight home instead of going for coffee with new acquaintances?

What are the defining moments of your life? What could have happened if you turned left at the stop light instead of right? Chosen one course of study over another, one college over another?

The goal of this memoir is to help you put your own life-defining moments into perspective. They have equipped you with the tools for survival in tumultuous times. They have made you who you are.

I suggest you use those events as opportunities for reflection and thanksgiving. We are alive. We're breathing, living and able to meet each day with gratitude or disdain. I will always choose gratitude over disdain, joy over sadness, triumph over tragedy and living over death—both physical and spiritual.

# 1

## Kept By Grace

Although I'm an early riser, the morning of July 17, 1971, started early, even for me. Something disturbed my sleep; something woke me up. The feeling of dread was so powerful, so overwhelming that I called my sister Thyra at about 5 o'clock in the morning. "Are the kids alright? Are the boys in the house?" My nephews were teenagers and it would not have been unusual for them to defy authority and break curfew by staying out all night. All was right in her house. With no apparent sign of disorder in my home or my sister's, I got ready for work.

The dread hung over my head all day long even at work at WBEE Radio in Harvey, just outside Chicago. I simply could not shake it. I kept asking my co-workers, "Are you alright? How's your family?" I called several friends whom I hadn't spoken with in ages and asked them the same. "Are you alright? How's your family?" I must have sounded like a possessed parrot, repeating the same questions over and over again.

During my four-hour show as "Merri Dee the Honeybee," the dread continued to buzz in my ears. It stalked me through my night gig back in Chicago at WSNS-TV and lurked in the wings as I finished my television talk show. Little did I know that after I left the TV studio, the drama of a lifetime would unfold.

At the end of my 8 p.m. hour-long show, a gentleman who had been a guest on another station program asked to speak with me about appearing on my talk show. He, his assistant and I decided to continue our conversation over coffee at a diner down the street. Since my car was parked in front of the station, I suggested I drive. After coffee, we returned to the station so that they could retrieve their cars. As the guest and I watched his assistant get into her car, I saw a man walking toward us. He had the build and complexion of one of the station's producers who lived in the neighborhood, so I paid him no attention.

"Open the door, or I'll shoot him," were the first words this mysterious man said to me as he pointed a shiny silver gun through the two-inch opening of the passenger's side window.

I obeyed. He got into the car on the passenger side, and told me to drive. The three of us were crammed into the front seat of my salmon-colored Mark III when we pulled out onto the street. I drove about two blocks when he instructed me to pull over. He spoke briefly to another man who approached the car from the shadows. "Butch, I got her," he said. "I'll meet you there," the man from the shadows replied. Clearly, the gunman had an accomplice. This was not some random act of violence, but a planned event. A planned kidnapping? They knew who I was. What do I do now?

Following the gunman's instructions, I turned left, turned right, traveled down busy streets and side streets, heading to the expressway. Stopping at a red light, I noticed a police car in the lane next to mine—officers who routinely patrolled the area. Normally, I would smile and offer some greeting, but not this time. When an officer said with a smile, "How are you doing?" I didn't respond. Trying to signal distress with my eyes and desperately hoping for some untapped psychic ability, I mentally pleaded with the officers for assistance. None came. The red light turned green, and again the gunman brandished the pistol to frighten us. It worked. We were afraid. The TV guest's body shook uncontrollably.

We entered the expressway going south and eventually we exited at 130th Street and arrived at Beaubian Woods, a part of the Cook County Forest Preserve. The gunman ordered both of us out of the car. The TV guest tried to engage the gunman in conversation in an attempt to change his mind. The guest then ran into the wooded area, while I considered knocking the pistol from the gunman's hand.

As I exited the car, I stumbled and lost one shoe. The gunman leaned down and picked it up and gave it to me. I remember the shooter's orders to the TV guest to stop where he was, then he led me to the same spot. He ordered both of us to get down on the ground—all the way on the ground. I remember my outrage. I had to get home to call my baby girl, let the dog out, and here I was lying on the ground in my brand new white silk suit, with one shoe on and one shoe off, my head in the mud messing up my makeup. Now, I know this is not your typical reaction while being threatened with a gun, but it was an angry woman's reaction.

I particularly remember the gunman's last words to me that evening. As I shivered on the wet ground, feeling cold, despite the warm and humid night, I heard him say, "I told you, I'm not going to hurt you." He lied!

# 2

## Fighting Back

I heard the first gunshot, followed by a heavy sigh. I felt the second shot hit me in the back of my head, and thought, "Oh, wow, this guy is going to kill us." A third shot rang out to my right. The gunman then pressed the .38-caliber revolver to the base of my neck and pulled the trigger. The fourth shot lit up my spine as though it was on fire.

In the heavy moments that followed, I realized that I'm not dead. I'm still alive. I lay very still, confused about being alive, yet grateful for this miracle. I reached out to touch the TV guest, who lay nearby, and proclaimed, "I'm alive! I'm alive! Don't worry, I'm going to get help."

It's a cliché to say the silence was the loudest I've ever heard, but it really was. Through the silence's deafening roar, I didn't hear a thing. I didn't hear the shooter walk away. I couldn't hear the cars rush by on the expressway. I didn't hear the TV guest make any sounds. Voiceless, I fervently prayed, "Dear God, help me, guide me. Let this guy get out of here so I can help this man next to me." The prayers continued until I heard a sound like a roaring ocean.

When you read about near death experiences, the most common description of the experience is being surrounded by a great white light, while hearing a James-Earl-Jones-type baritone voice offering words of comfort. That was not quite my experience. Instead of a great white light, I heard the roar of the ocean and saw an ocean wave form, building and growing larger with every passing moment until it formed a corridor over me. I experienced an overwhelming feeling of comfort and peace, accompanied by the rhythmic sounds of the ocean.

What happened next takes me back to my childhood as the youngest of six on Chicago's South Side. In the evening after everyone was supposed to be in bed, occasionally my dad would come through, checking on his kids after hearing us whispering and giggling. Dad was our everything after our mother died. He was the stability in our lives, the calming presence in a chaotic world. As he walked down the hallway toward our bedroom, one of my sisters, probably Thyra, would say," Shhhh, here comes Jesus." It was meant to be a private bit of silly humor, comparing Dad to the Savior. As kids, we found it very funny. But years later, on that warm July night, the private joke shared among sisters now meant so much more.

As I lay on the ground, I saw a vision of this tall, thin man riding the waves effortlessly and smoothly, as if on a skateboard. Was this Jesus? Or my dad, who  was also tall, thin and very regal? The man glided slowly until he was right in front of me and said, "It's OK, it's OK. You can go back. You'll be fine. You can go back." The man turned and glided back in the direction from which he came and the corridor began to unfurl until he disappeared.

As his image faded, so did the sound of the ocean. The surrounding sounds of the July night returned. Still unmoving, I could hear the sound of car tires on the expressway. I could hear the cicadas in the woods, but I couldn't hear the gunman. Had he left? Or was he nearby waiting to finish what he had started?

I had no answers, but I had to get going. I pushed with my arms and hands to get up and couldn't. I crawled on my hands and knees to my left, the way I came into this forest. I had to get back to the expressway. If I made it back to the main road, there was a chance that someone would see me and help us. So like a baby finding her way, I crawled and crawled. It seemed like forever.

Dying in the woods just yards away from civilization was not an option I wanted to accept. I saw a flashing light of a railroad trestle on a side road that ran parallel to the expressway. I tried focusing on the flashing light, using it as a guide, but my vision went in and out of focus. I stopped only to periodically wipe my eyes. Although I didn't realize it at the time, my face was covered with mud mixed with the blood streaming from my head. What a mess I must have been!

Inch by inch, moment by moment, I eventually made it to that side road, but I was still a long way from safety. I saw the headlights from a car driving toward the place the gunman had left us. I thought, "Oh my God, I have to crawl back to where he shot me so he won't know I'm alive."

I crawled back to that horrid spot where I felt the first bullet entry and I lay there, holding my breath and praying that the driver would not stop, that he would not get out of the car. The car stopped on the side of the road and I waited for what seemed like an eternity. Then it finally drove off.

I remember feeling intense fear. And I recalled what my dad told me: "Fear is false evidence appearing real." Not wanting to give in to this false evidence, I struggled to my knees and crawled back to the road. I flailed my arms trying to flag down some help from the passing cars on the expressway. None stopped. Amazing.

But then something miraculous happened. As a private ambulance sped past me, it suddenly was rear-ended by a woman driving a car behind it. The woman's husband was a patient inside the ambulance on his way to the hospital. Ironically, this woman spotted me when others didn't or chose to ignore me, and she took action. Once the vehicles pulled to the shoulder, the woman ordered the ambulance driver to put her husband into her car—she would take him to the hospital herself. She then instructed the driver to go back and give me assistance. I don't know that woman's name, but I am forever grateful for her presence, mindfulness and charity.

As you can imagine, the next moments and intervals were kaleidoscopically chaotic. Like a nightmare moving in and out of perception, events and people swirled around me. It was a nauseating procession of faces, voices and sounds. Some were helpful, some were obstacles and still others were just there. The ambulance driver refused to get out of the driver's seat, as he quoted regulations against picking up anyone from the side of the road, and left me to his newly hired assistant. The assistant, who seemed embarrassed by his partner's behavior, tried to help and put either towels or a blanket around me. It had rained recently, and the smell of wet earth clung to my nostrils.

The blessed silence was quickly replaced by a cacophony of sounds: police sirens, whizzing cars, the loud racket of cicadas from the nearby forest preserve, and the offbeat chatter of the ambulance driver and his assistant as they questioned me. Their voices battered my senses, but I had to stay focused to get the help I needed.

As I sat shivering at the side of the ambulance, all I could think to say was that a man who needed help was over there just past that big boulder. While trying to explain, I saw the blue lights of a police car and breathed a sigh of relief. I thought, real help had arrived. The officer exited his car and walked toward us.

He questioned me about what happened. He then told the ambulance driver to go into the forest to find the TV guest and bring him out. He took my arm and led me to the police car and suggested I lean on the side of the car and that someone would come for me. I was too muddy and bloody I guess to sit inside. I heard him on his radio saying he was off duty or going to be off duty soon. It sounded like he was rushing them to get him the help he needed so he could leave.

When they returned with the TV guest on the stretcher, the officer told them to take him to the hospital. At this moment I wanted to fuss, but those early lessons from Dad about being obedient, ladylike and quiet came rushing back. I leaned against the squad car for as long as I could and then I slid to the ground while he continued to question me about what had happened. "Who was the man? Who was with me in the car? Where was the gun?"

It seemed as though there were a thousand questions before I saw a blue light. Yay! It was a patrol wagon! He reached down and helped me up. It felt like he only did that so no one would know that he had left me on the ground to fend for myself. They put me on a stretcher, laid me on the floor of the patrol wagon and off we went. I remember the stretcher slamming against the walls or seats as the patrol wagon whizzed around the corners. My head felt like it was exploding.

In the hospital, there were more questions from doctors as they prepped me for assessment, questions from a police sergeant and a Chicago Daily News reporter, all asking me, "Where is my gun?" I was so confused. What gun? I did not have a gun. Soon the realization struck me like a lightning bolt that the sergeant and the reporter were implying that the shooter and I were together. I screamed! My head pounded! The doctors stopped the questions and kicked everyone out. The hospital staff then spoke softly to me, trying to calm me down. At last, help for me had truly arrived.

A life-changing moment takes practically all of your emotional, spiritual and sometimes physical reserves to survive. It is a moment that forces you to determine who you are or are not. It forces you to determine what you will or will not accept, and makes you choose how you will respond.

Some relatives, loved ones, friends and associates have told me that my treatment at the hands of these officials was nothing less than callous indifference, if not outright meanness. Others have described those moments as raw ignorance or a sad sign of the times. They probably are all correct. South Chicago Community Hospital was located in an all-black neighborhood on Chicago's South Side. The patrol wagon bypassed at least two other hospitals that normally served white patients to take me to the one that served a predominately black clientele.

I don't dwell on the racism aspect of the situation. Was it racism? Was it heartless indifference? I chose not to participate in that discussion because my focus was on much more than race. My concern was survival. I chose to focus on that. My life lesson was clear. It was about acceptance, forgiveness and gratitude.

# 3

# My Life-Changing Moment

## By Toya Campbell

My mom can talk about forgiveness, acceptance and life's defining moments, but I was 13 and that first moment I learned about the kidnapping and shooting turned my life upside down. I'll never forget it. The details never diminish. That moment flipped a switch in my life. I went from being a 13-year-old kid to a 13-year-old adult. There was no time for self-doubt, self-recriminations, or even fear, although as expected, I was very afraid.

I was on vacation in California visiting my uncle, aunt and cousin. We had spent a normal day playing in the sunshine, hanging with friends and swimming. After returning home and finishing dinner, one of the first things I remember was the moment I realized that Mom hadn't called. It was 9 at night and I hadn't heard from her. That was so unusual. We talked every night, no matter what. Wherever she was, Mom always took a moment to call me. So I called her. No answer. I waited about an hour and called again; again no answer. Now I was scared.

Uncle Buster tried to calm me, saying that Mom was probably out for the evening and she would call me in the morning. I didn't buy his explanation for a moment. About 11 p.m., Aunt Thyra called with the news of the kidnapping and shooting. She gave us all the information she had, which frankly, wasn't enough for me.

Even today, I can almost hear the click of that switch—the realization of my worst fears and the end of my childhood as I knew it.

Uncle Buster and Aunt Odessa encouraged me to wait by saying, "We'll know more in the morning." The unspoken thoughts in my head challenged all of their "waiting" rationales. "Wait for what? Wait for her to die? What am I supposed to wait for?" I immediately packed my suitcase, called the airline and waited for the cab I called. I was on my way home to Chicago, to my mother.

Imagine a 13-year-old, who had just received the worst news of her life, in possession of a return airline ticket, packed bags, and enough money for cab fare for both ends of the trip. And don't forget this same 13-year-old was being reared by a self-determined, self-possessed single parent, who had taught her daughter to look at life straight on without blinking. This was the person who stood before my uncle and aunt when the cab driver arrived. Sizing up the look on my face, Uncle Buster instructed the driver to wait, while he quickly packed his own suitcase and accompanied me on the flight back home and then directly to the hospital.

*My Life Changing Moment*

The hospital bed seemed to swallow Mom. She was alive, but blind and paralyzed. Bandages covered her head and portions of her face. She was so defenseless and helpless that I had to take control.

With the help of my cousin Karen, who was only a few years older, I made medical decisions, vetted the visitors list, obtained security, handled the media and kept our many relatives calm and focused. No one would expect a 13-year-old to handle such responsibilities today, and frankly, no one expected it back then, either. But I did what had to be done. My mom was depending on me.

There was a moment when the gravity of the situation delivered a straight-arm power punch directly to my gut. The doctors held a family conference to discuss the benefits and drawbacks of performing surgery to remove one of the bullets from Mom's brain. We listened to their explanations and looked at the X-rays and drawings they provided. The doctors told us, "If we operate to remove the bullets, she may wake up paralyzed and blind. But if we do nothing, the bullets may shift and she still might end up paralyzed and blind." The conversation paused as everyone awaited my decision. Some family members wailed and cried at this news. Others sat stoically silent. I briefly consulted my cousin Karen and a few other relatives, then made the decision—no operation. I said to myself, "What have I done? How could I make such a critical decision?"

Dignitaries and public figures streamed in and out of the hospital. The Rev. Jesse Jackson performed last rites on more than one occasion. Through it all, I rarely left Mom's side. Even though doctors said she couldn't hear me, I talked to her constantly. "Mommy, you can't die," I pleaded. "Mommy you promised me. You said you'd never leave me. You said it was just the two of us. You said we were best girlfriends. Mommy you've got to get better. Mommy you can't die."

# 4
## Moving On

I was not aware of all the people, events and forces that surrounded me as I fought for my life and my ability to see and move. I've been told that after a few days in the hospital, I responded to Toya's voice, but I couldn't do much else.

Nationally, only about 5 percent of victims with gunshots to the head survive, according to recent statistics. I'm sure the survival rate in 1971 was much worse. I was one of the rare survivors. What was particularly upsetting though, was the way the criminal justice system treated me afterward. I wasn't permitted to testify at my kidnapper's trial. I was prevented from allowing my personal attorney to represent my interests in the proceedings. Instead, the Cook County State's Attorney's Office represented me.

The kidnapper and gunman, Samuel Drew, was eventually captured, tried and imprisoned for the kidnapping and murder of the TV guest; my kidnapping and attempted murder; out of state theft (because he was found in Indiana in my car with the gun on the seat); and several other charges related to that evening. He received a term of 120 years, but he only served 12 years.

When Drew was released from prison, the authorities did not notify me about his release to ensure my safety. I felt as if I was on my own—and I was. I only learned that he was out of prison when a neighbor told me that he was back in Chicago.

Here I am, a 34-year-old woman who miraculously survived a shooting. After weeks in the hospital, my life was spared. Now, I asked myself: "What are you going to do for this world? How are you going to prevent other victims of gun violence from learning about their assailants release—by word of mouth?" I dedicated myself to advocating for victims' rights. In 1986 I testified before the National Sentencing Commission on behalf of victims of violence and families of those who could no longer speak.

Working with Jesse White, who then served in the Illinois General Assembly (currently Illinois Secretary of State), I witnessed the passage of the state's first Victims Bill of Rights. It served as a model for similar laws throughout the United States. It was such a proud moment. I had been the catalyst for a bill that would eventually serve to change lives in the United States of America.

It wasn't easy to do, and it was painful recalling how I was left to die. But it had to be done and I had to do it. The law mandates that a victim of an extremely violent crime would receive some form of notification when the assailant is released.

Since the events of 7-17-71, I'm often asked about being afraid to die. I've seen death, stared it in the eyes, talked with Jesus about it, and I am not afraid. Not anymore.

*Moving On*

There are two events in your life over which you have no control—the day you're born and the day you die. What happens between those two days are the only times where you can exercise some control. The choices you make determine whether those days are ones filled with gratitude or despair. I chose gratitude.

To get you from despair to gratitude, I want you to answer a question my grandfather asked me, "What are you going to do for this world?" He didn't care if you were a student in seventh grade, he wanted to know about your plans to share your time, talent or treasure, because there was always something you could do and there was always someone in need.

Ask yourself, "Who can I help?" Perhaps it's a neighbor or a youngster you know. Helping someone else is a great way of taking your mind off of your own problems. Ask yourself, "How can I right some wrong?" It won't be easy. You may get discouraged but you must push on. Your choice is your responsibility. Remember these 10 little two-letter words, which always motivate me: "If it is to be, it is up to me."

# 5

## When Hollywood Calls

I am forever grateful for the love and concern shown to me after the kidnapping and shooting. People sent bushel baskets of cards and letters telling me how much they missed seeing me on TV or hearing me on my radio show. I appreciated their prayers and good wishes. I know they led to my recovery.

I applaud my fellow media colleagues for championing my story. Essence ran a compelling story on my life after the shooting. Harry Reasoner interviewed me on "60 Minutes." Working with the "60 Minutes" producers helped me remember the details of that night and see the impact my story had on the nation.

The extensive national media coverage prompted about five calls from Hollywood, including one from Dick Clark, who wanted to produce a film on my life. But the call that caught my attention was from Jim Brown, the ex-Cleveland Browns football star. He read the Essence article and told his friend Richard Pryor that my story would make a great movie. Richard had recently inked an unprecedented $40 million deal to produce movies for Columbia Pictures. Jim and Richard's deal with Columbia included a partnership with Motown's film division. Motown had moved into the movie world with Diana Ross' film debut in "Lady Sings the Blues," followed by "Mahogany" and "The Wiz."

Jim told me that the story of my survival was so life-changing and inspiring that I simply had to share it with the world. At first I shuddered because I knew the privacy I enjoyed would be over. But I agreed that my story could help others. I clearly understood the power of prayer and how it can lead to miracles. I wanted to celebrate that truth in the movie.

The next thing I knew, I was on a plane headed to Hollywood. I met with Suzanne DePasse, head of Motown's film division, and other execs. The talk was Diana Ross would play my part. That was fine with me. Then in one of our meetings, the film project turned into a possible TV "Movie of the Week."

Motown had a script written. Things were moving in the right direction. I called my friend Nancy

Wilson, who happened to be performing in Chicago, and told her the good news. "There's a TV movie in the works on me," I said. "Phylicia Rashad from 'The Cosby Show' might portray me." Nancy was thrilled. I was thrilled with the possibility of it all.

However, everything changed when I read the script. I didn't see Merri Dee anywhere in that script. It was not my story. I know Hollywood can take a little poetic license, but this just went too far. The script focused on a black woman kidnapped with a white man. Remember, the incident happened in 1971 when race relations and black awareness were the topics of the day. The Black Power movement was in full swing. Nina Simone wrote and recorded "To Be Young, Gifted and Black." Aretha Franklin later recorded her own soulful rendition of the tune on her 1972 album "Young, Gifted and Black."

The script dealt with the relevant issues of those times. I understood all that. But what happened to my story, my voice? It was not the story I envisioned.

I wasn't comfortable with signing away the rights to my life story, to my legacy, to the brand name of Merri Dee. My attorney advised me not to sign. It was giving away my power. I don't think I would have had any rights to change anything. Also, it really wasn't much money. I think it was about $35,000. I didn't need the money. I needed to keep my pride and dignity. I could not sell out. I never wanted that type of fame, anyway. I realized it was about more than me. I represented a lot of people during an era of change. Motown and I agreed to disagree.

I have always been grateful for Motown's interest. I learned a lot about the movie industry. That time spent was invaluable. My spirit remains open to a movie, perhaps on network or cable TV if the right script comes along.

My lesson to you is quite simple. Don't sell your soul. Follow your inner voice. Pray for guidance and wisdom. Trust that things will work out as they should, when they should, the way they should. Be strong, bold and clear in your decisions. If you do, you will not have any regrets.

# 6

## Just As I Am

Agnes Blouin already had five children ranging in age from 5 to 13 when she returned to Chicago from New Orleans on the Illinois Central's Panama Limited. The train ride was supposed to be just another trip between her roots and her new home—one that she'd made several times before. Sometimes Agnes traveled with her husband, John, or sometimes with her twin sister, Naomi. As always, the plan was that she would disembark at Chicago's 12th Street Station and take a streetcar home.

But this time was different. First of all, Agnes was very pregnant. Second, it was October 30, the day before Halloween, in the middle of the Great Depression. Somewhere between southern Illinois and the 12th Street Station, she went into labor. Somehow, she made it home to 5640 S. Indiana Avenue in Chicago, where I was born about four minutes before midnight, four minutes before Halloween, the youngest child of John and Agnes Blouin.

I was given the name Mary Frances, after my maternal grandmother, but I've been called many names throughout the years: "The Voice," "Merri Dee the Honeybee," "Beloved," and even some unflattering ones, like "Monkey Face." I've held many titles. I am a mother, grandmother, sister, aunt, cousin, daughter, wife, ex-wife, daughter-in-law, adoptive mother, mentor, neighbor, concerned community resident, survivor, colleague, motivator and friend. I've been a bag girl in a grocery store, computer demonstrator, runway model, auto show commentator, disc jockey, newscaster, radio and TV talk show host, editorial spokesperson, mistress/master of ceremonies, broadcast administrator, AARP Illinois state president, commissioner on the Illinois Human Rights Commission, U.S. Army Ambassador, successful fundraiser, adoption advocate, children's champion and one of Chicago's first African-American females in the broadcast business.

But all of those identities and roles began as Mary Frances. As a child, my siblings and neighborhood kids called me "Skinny" and "Skinny Minny" because I was so thin, a stiff wind could blow me over. The nickname never really bothered me because in my heart, I knew those taunts weren't directed at me. "Skinny" wasn't my name. My name was Mary Frances.

Each of us is given a name shortly after we're born. That name represents something special. Sometimes it's the name of a dear relative—as in my case—or maybe it's an expression of a parent's creativity. Regardless of a family's wealth or level of need, that name is precious. It reflects the dignity bestowed upon us by our parents.

*Just As I Am*

After my mother died when I was 2, my father sold the family home and moved my youngest brother, Alphonse, and me into the home of a woman named Esther, who later became my stepmother. Although she never took my father's last name (I'll tell you more about that later), she called me names much worse than "Skinny Minny."

Her favorite name for me was "Monkey Face." As a child, the Monkey Face insult hurt my feelings, but what deeply wounded me was the time she used a derogatory label for me, taking advantage of my naïveté. It was when I was in fifth grade with my favorite teacher, Mrs. Robinson. We had a homework assignment to think about what we wanted to be when we grew up. That's a normal question to ask a child.

At home, I told Esther about the assignment. It was one of the rare occasions when she was acting nice to me. I said, "I don't know what I want to be when I grow up," but I was actually thinking about being a nurse or someone who works with animals, because I always liked dogs.

She replied in a matter-of-fact manner, "Oh, you'll probably be a whore when you grow up." Not knowing the meaning of the word whore and not knowing any better, I accepted her answer as a viable career choice.

The next day in class, all the students eagerly shared their dreams and goals. Some wanted to be a teacher like Mrs. Robinson. Somebody wanted to be mailman. (Remember postal workers didn't come along as a career choice for both boys and girls until much later.) Several boys wanted to be policemen. Lots of girls wanted to be housewives and mothers. One or two students wanted to be movie stars. As Mrs. Robinson stood in the front of the class, I raised my hand. She asked, "Mary Frances, what do you want to be when you grow up?" Gazing up into my teacher's eyes, with all the innocence of an unknowing child, I answered, "I'm going to be a whore when I grow up."

The momentary silence was quickly broken by

the sound of the other students laughing at me. As tears welled in her eyes, Mrs. Robinson called me to the front of the class and took me out in the hallway. She said, "I want you to go to the library, look up every word that sounds like whore, write it down, and bring it back to me." It wasn't hard. Along with the expected definition, I found horehound, like the cough drops by Smith Brothers. That totally confused me. Was I going to be a cough drop when I grew up? Or maybe I'd work in a cough drop factory.

Actually, the time spent in the library looking up that definition was time well spent. Seeing other words allowed me to imagine all kinds of occupations and possibilities. Later, Mrs. Robinson made me stay after class and said, "You will not be a whore. You're a fine young lady, and you will grow up to be somebody very, very special." How did she know?

Names have power. And calling someone out of their name, as the old folks used to say, can transform people and situations. That's why the ability to name someone or to take away someone's name exerts a very powerful influence on someone's identity. Esther exercised that type of power when she had my name legally changed to her last name. When I tell others of this incident, many are outraged, disbelieving that it actually occurred. They ask questions like, "How could she do that? Or why did she do that?" Or they express indignation at the legal system, as if that mattered. I was a child, so the legal details are unclear. I am clear that her last name is on my high school diploma from Chicago's Englewood High School.

Having my name changed was one of the most hurtful experiences. It robbed me of my very essence as an individual.

The power she exerted over my life only intensified when she changed my name. One of the first things she did was to forbid my family—siblings, aunts, uncles, grandparents, cousins—from having any contact with me. The second thing she did was to send me about a thousand miles away from home when I was 12 to a cloistered convent and girls' school in New Orleans. Once at St. Mary's Academy for Girls, I no longer had any contact with my family or the outside world, even though a few of my relatives lived in the family's home state of Louisiana and in the city of New Orleans. She gave the sisters at St. Mary's strict orders. I was not allowed to leave the convent grounds, except for school events. I was not allowed to walk with my classmates to the nearby park or shop at a local store. I was not allowed to have visitors. I was not allowed to return to

Chicago for holiday breaks. I was left alone with the nuns.

Years later, after demonstrating new computers for IBM and modeling in Chicago, I decided to go back to school. I majored in broadcast engineering at the Midwestern School of Broadcasting, now Columbia College Chicago. As a young girl, some called me a tomboy because I enjoyed watching the neighborhood boys while they worked on their cars or tinkered with small electronics. I could take anything apart and put it back together with the best of them. At college it seemed only natural for me to focus on engineering.

*Just As I Am*

Even though I focused on engineering, I studied broadcasting at the suggestion of a professor. Soon, other students and instructors were dropping in on my classes to hear me speak. That was when I was given the pet name, "The Voice," and professors began to push me into radio and TV.

Instructors told me that I would have few opportunities in engineering, particularly as an African-American female. One professor said, "The industry is not ready for you yet." He was trying to be kind and realistic, not discouraging. He wanted to spare me disappointment. Even with his words in my ears, I still tried to find engineering positions. Need I tell you that a career in broadcast engineering was not in my future?

Instead, "The Voice" secured a disc jockey position at WBEE Radio in Harvey, Illinois, making me one of the country's first African-American female broadcasters. The year was 1966 and at WBEE was where the handle "Merri Dee the Honeybee" became my radio persona.

Dr. Chan, one of my professors, once told me that my married name, Mary Dorham, did not have enough pizzazz for radio. "Shorten it to Dee," he advised. "Since you are always so happy and upbeat, your name should reflect that." I followed his advice, changed the spelling of my first name to Merri (a play on the word "merry") and Merri Dee was born.

The year 1966 was an exciting time to be in the media. Chicago Mayor Richard J. Daley was at the helm. Dr. Martin Luther King, Jr. came to the city, moved into a Lawndale apartment and marched in Marquette Park. Based in Chicago, the Rev. Jesse Jackson worked closely with Dr. King in the Civil Rights Movement. The Vietnam War was in full swing. Race riots were jumping off across the country. The Beatles kicked off a U.S. tour in Chicago. What would have significance for me later: Richard Speck murdered eight nurses in the dormitory at a South Side hospital. It was a tumul-

Life
Lessons On
Faith,
Forgiveness
& Grace
᭞᭞᭞᭞᭞

tuous time. Other black female broadcasters of that era, Carole Simpson, Yvonne Daniels and one or two others in gospel, were on the front row of the cultural transformation that was taking place. We were the voices of our communities.

My radio persona attracted a growing following during my first year. A friend suggested that I look into doing a TV show to promote my radio work. It sounded like a good idea. I walked boldly into the reception area of WCIU-TV and asked to see the general manager. With no appointment and not enough of a radio following to impress the receptionist, I was politely invited to return once I had an appointment.

I later returned and was given my first television show, "The Merri Dee Show," which I produced, hosted and secured sponsorships. My guests were friends made during my time on radio, such as Nancy Wilson, Cannonball Adderley and Ramsey Lewis. My very first guests were the comedy duo Tim and Tom. They went on to become the multitalented performers of TV and film. Tim Reid won fame on the hit TV series, "WKRP In Cincinnati" and Tom Dressen went on the road with Frank Sinatra as his opening act.

I have learned that my broadcast name, Merri Dee,

truly defines me. It is a strong and trusted brand name that represents class, elegance, strength and survival. What you call yourself and what you allow others to call you certainly assists in defining who you are.

In talking with young people, I often hear about incidents in which someone said something negative about someone else—the usual he-said, she-said drama that goes on in school. I always ask, "Is that statement true?" Is the name you're being called your name, the name you received at birth?" That's when I tell the young person (usually a teenage girl) to "hold your head up high and throw your shoulders back." If it's not your name, don't answer to it. If the words are less than kind and cause hurt or discomfort, consider dropping that relationship. After all, it's your name and your reputation at stake.

Likewise, if someone calls you "Beloved," "Cherished," "My Cheri," "Sweetie," "My Boo" or other terms of endearment or respect, embrace that relationship. Be keenly aware, however, that there are people who will call you sweet names attempting to catch you off guard. But even then, don't be gullible. Be aware.

# 7

# Defining Moments Revisited

Defining moments can be great or small, dramatic or modest. Such moments force us to examine our values, our hopes and our beliefs. They crystallize who we are.

If you've read this far, you already know about one of the most dramatically defining moments of my life—the kidnapping and shooting. My life has been full of these moments, and not all have been traumatic. In fact, I don't view my life as a tragedy. My life is a miracle.

Looking back, I can pinpoint the significant events that have transformed me into the woman I am today, including September 11, my first day in radio, my trip to South Africa, and of course, the birth of my daughter.

## September 11, 2001

It's about 8:30 in the morning. I am on United Airlines Flight 602 preparing to land at Reagan International Airport in Washington, D.C. for a National Tree Trustee Board meeting. Aroused from a light sleep, I open my eyes, raise the airplane's window shade and peer outside. As the plane begins its descent, the passengers hear the pilot say, "Oh my God. Oh my God. Oh my God. There's been a plane crash. A plane has just flown into the World Trade Center." Suddenly, we feel the plane change direction and begin to rise again. There's a man sitting next to me on the aisle, he is sound asleep.

Thoughts rush through my mind—the World Trade Center in New York? How could they do that? The entire situation seems so surreal. I try to put a rational spin on the situation. Perhaps the New York pilot passed out or had a heart attack. Then our pilot's voice again comes through the speakers: "They've just closed the airport, and we're diverting to Dulles Airport."

Dulles Airport? As many times as I have flown into Washington, I had never landed at Dulles Airport. I had no idea where it was or how far it was from D.C. From my window view, I can see the plane is making a wide turn when the pilot says, "Oh my God. Oh my God!" And then dead silence.

I elbow my sleeping neighbor in the side and shout, "Wake up!" He continues to doze. "You've got to wake up. Wake up!" Still drowsy, he finally opens his eyes and looks at me as if I'm crazy. Actually, I can't blame him because this is our first real encounter—my elbow in his ribs. I continue, "Did you hear the pilot? Did you hear what he said?"

Calmly, and I must say too calmly, the man responds as if he is reciting the multiplication tables. "A plane has crashed into the World Trade Center. We're diverting. We're going to another airport." After a brief pause, he says "OK?"

*Defining Moments Revisited*

And the first thing that hits me is, "Oh my God. I'm sitting next to somebody who did this." The word "terrorism" doesn't enter my thinking, but something just isn't right about him. I slide as close to the window as possible and don't look at him again.

The plane continues to bank and turn. Another plane passes us very closely. Later, we find out American Airlines Flight 77 from Dulles Airport in Virginia was hijacked and crashed into the Pentagon. After landing, the flight attendant instructs us to form a line, take all of our belongings and quickly get off the plane. "Don't go to baggage claim," she says. Fortunately, for me, I only have my purse and an overnight bag.

Anyone who has ever been on a landing plane has heard the announcement to remain seated until the aircraft comes to a complete stop. This time, nobody—not the pilot, copilot or flight attendants—says anything about remaining seated. As soon as the wheels touch down, passengers grab their belongings. I glance at my seatmate, sitting there with his left hand on his chin, calmly looking at people. More than anything else, his peaceful demeanor in the midst of panic raises the hairs on my arm. He scares the heck out of me.

Everyone exits the plane with me in the mix. I hear an urgent public address announcement: "Get out of the airport. Get out of the airport. Do not pick up luggage. Do not pick up luggage. Get out of the airport." I trail behind the crowd, wondering what to do next. My bladder and nerves make the decision for me. I have to go. I must find a bathroom or, well, you get the picture.

I run into the bathroom and take less than two minutes to use the toilet without washing my hands. I always wash my hands, but frantic times call for frantic measures. I run back out. I look left, no one. I look right, no one. There was a crowd of people here just moments ago. A thick feeling rises in my throat. Which way is out? I stand stock still struggling to remember. I replay my steps—got off the plane, turned right to the restroom. Or did I turn left? I recall people running and screaming. I tell myself, "Just be calm. Don't panic. You can't panic because you don't do that well. You're not good at that. Just be calm." I close my eyes, asking, "Which way do I go?" I hear an inner voice say, "Run to your right." I take off running to my right—in high heels, huffing and puffing, losing my breath because I'm not a runner.

In the distance, I see two women in uniform crying and hugging each other. As I approach, I ask, "Am I going the right way to get out?" One of the women points. Yes! I am headed in the right direction, so I keep running until I hear the sounds of people and end up just outside of the terminal. There on the inner tarmac is a shuttle bus with a rear opening for loading luggage. People are scrambling to get on board. The bus begins to move out and I hear a man say, "Jump, run, jump. We'll catch you. Hurry up, jump." Throwing my purse and overnight bag ahead of me, I jump onboard.

I am frightened out of my mind. But then I remember, "I'm Merri Dee. I must get things done. I must come through." That is my constant refrain. But it's not just about me. This is an emergency and I must help." But all I know to do is pray. "Dear God, please

*Defining
Moments
Revisited*

let everything be all right," I plead with my hands tightly clasped on my lap. "Please help people stop crying."

The panic on the shuttle bus is even worse than on the plane. When the bus stops at the main terminal, people rush out. Inside the terminal, some passengers run. Others collapse on the floor, crying and holding each other.

Near me stands a tall, thin man using a walkie-talkie. He notices me looking at him. I turn my head to avoid looking at him, and then briskly walk toward the exit. A voice calls out, "Miss Dee. Miss Dee."

I think, "Oh my God, he knows me. How does he know me?" I refuse to look his way. I am so scared. I lower my voice and snap, "Who wants to know?" As the man approaches, he replies, "I'm security for the Cardinal in Chicago." Here is a member of his security detail who I thought might be a terrorist. He was not a terrorist, but a godsend coming to my aid.

It turns out, he is on the walkie-talkie speaking to someone in White House security. The information is not good. By this time, American Flight 77 has crashed into the Pentagon and another plane has not answered hails and has dropped from radar. Suddenly, he says, "We have to get out of here."

Outside the terminal, all cars, buses and cabs are at a standstill. Some sit empty, abandoned by their drivers. In the distance, we see the taillights of rows and rows of vehicles trying to exit the airport. For the second time that day, I run, this time with the Cardinal's security person. We eventually catch up to a van with a group of women who were on our flight—the Republican Women of Illinois. One of the women says, "Miss Dee. Merri Dee, we wondered where you went. We want to take you with us. There's a bus coming to get us." I send silent prayers of thanksgiving for sending these angels to rescue us.

During the 12-hour trip back home, we sing hymns, pray and cry. A silence overtakes everyone as the bus passes the Pennsylvania field where United Flight 93 crashed. We look on the burned and blackened ground. We pray, some cry quietly.

To say September 11, 2001 was a redefining moment for me and the entire nation is an understatement. Most people remember exactly where they were when they first heard about the attacks. This incident brought back the emotions surrounding my kidnapping and shooting. Here I was again, in a similar situation, desperate to survive. I triumphed. Once again, God demonstrated His enduring grace in my life.

### First Day in Radio

If I could use my gift of gab to support my daughter and myself, then that's what I was going to do. My first day on the air in radio was on WBEE in Harvey, just south of Chicago. That was where the radio signal was located, but I sat in a Dodge automobile showroom window in the inner city, decked out in a 10-gallon cowboy hat and full cowgirl regalia. I was a spectacle. I drew plenty of attention.

There I was, spinning records, reading commercials, interviewing customers live on the air and waving at the cars whizzing down the boulevard. It was fun, plus the gig paid well. What more could I ask for at 30 years of age?

Who knew dressing up as a cowgirl would jump-start a star-studded, 43-year broadcast career? To me, it was simply a job and I needed to work. I was divorced with a very young daughter and had resigned from a "good job" at IBM working with computers and traveling to be home with my child.

The life lesson here is to keep your eyes, ears, mind and heart open. Exciting things can happen when you try something different. Sometimes carefully daring to be different causes change to happen.

## Race and Work

Racism is like gravity. Its force can pull some people down or provide others with something to push against. When I felt that pull during my broadcast career, I pushed back harder. I remember my first day as a midday news anchor for WGN-TV in Chicago. It was a major career achievement and a major boost to my morale after my abduction and shooting 18 months earlier. I had been chosen out of 168. In fact, I was No. 168.

In those pre-teleprompter days, we read the news from sheets of paper. I'm sitting in the chair with my co-anchor, Jerry, who is at a separate desk. Lights are on, cameras are live, and I hear Jerry read a story about a woman who had been murdered in her home. When I heard the name of the person, at first I did and didn't hear it. That is your training. Then I realized, "Oh my God, Hazel Dorham, that is my mother-in-law!"

Although I had been divorced from her son for several years, Hazel and I had maintained a very friendly relationship. After all, she was my daughter's doting grandmother and they shared a close relationship. I broke down on camera, in front of hundreds of thousands of television viewers. Career suicide.

The writers didn't know that "Dorham" had been my married name and that I had a connection to

*Defining Moments Revisited*

Hazel. It was just a routine news story for the midday broadcast.

Some writers apologized, even though it wasn't their fault. My co-anchor handled my on-camera breakdown admirably and graciously expressed his sentiments. My news director and station manager offered their assistance.

But there were others who made unkind, racially insensitive comments or implied there was a connection between Hazel's murder and my kidnapping and shooting. I knew this was a defining moment in my career. I may have broken down on camera, but I didn't break. I was soon back in the anchor chair determined to get on with my work.

In many ways, my WGN career mirrored my life. Some moments were touching, some painful, some puzzling. I dealt with racists, sexists and outright malicious people. While I refuse to view my first newscast and the reactions of my colleagues in a racial light, there were other instances that can only be construed in that manner.

There was the engineer who, I believe, deliberately erased my sample reel, but denied it. And the news director who had problems with me because, as he put it, I "conveyed too much caring about the people" in the news stories. He also told me that I looked too young and wanted me to change my hair and dress to appear older. At the time, I was around 37 years old. Did he want me to look like his idea of a grandmother? Maybe he had a hard time determining the age of African-American women. It wasn't what he said, but how he said it. I later learned that he often made derogatory remarks about women and did not have a good relationship with his mother.

There were also the people who ignored me when I greeted them in the hallways. There were the times I found nasty notes on the windshield of my car. And when I first went on the air, the station was flooded with hostile calls from viewers furious that a woman of color was allowed to sit at the anchor desk. The WGN switchboard lit up like Michigan Avenue during Christmas.

Yet for every racist, sexist or cruel person I encountered, there were also charming and supportive people. I recall the gracious reception I received from Lee Phillip, a Chicago media powerhouse and the co-creator of several soap operas, including the long-running "The Young and the Restless."

"Keep your nose to the grindstone," she told me. "Remember they hired you because they needed you. You bring something. You may not know what that is right away, but you bring something special. Remember that. Take ownership of it and feel good about yourself. You'll get people trying to pull you down. There'll be many people who will try to negate what you're doing, but remember that you're good at what you do."

Lee Phillip reminded me that I deserved to be on the air. She offered me a guiding light. I never forgot her advice and I pass it on to you.

**Laughter and Humor**

Chicago is a sports town and WGN is a sports station. Merri Dee reporting sports in those early days is like Rodman wearing that wedding gown to promote his autobiography. An absolute spectacle. When I started at WGN, I knew little about sports, which was a big part of the anchor job. I would read a player's name wrong, then lose my place among the papers, or call an athlete by the wrong name, then fall out laughing at myself.

"Did I say his name was Henry Kissinger? Oh my goodness, that's not the right name. I meant Don Kessinger," I would say, laughing. Male viewers particularly got a kick out of my comic blunders, and I soon built a loyal following. Whenever I was in public, guys would say, "You are so funny. You say the wrong thing, and then you laugh at yourself. And we laugh too."

Ironically, the trait I considered a liability endeared me to Chicago viewers. I believe they excused my sports errors because I was a local girl who had "done good." People respected that I was hardworking, down-to-earth and a survivor—hallmarks of a true Chicagoan. I could laugh at my mistakes.

The ability to laugh at yourself, to see the humor in everyday situations is so important. It will help get you through the tough times.

*Defining Moments Revisited*

## Pregnancy, Childbirth and the Gift of Acceptance

I met a young man when we were in high school. He was smitten with me. His grandmother believed we would be good for each other and wanted us to marry. But I wasn't so sure. Still, we had a pleasant time together relieving the boredom of working and studying. In time, I became pregnant.

I was scared. I worked at a supermarket in the evenings and weekends and could barely feed myself, let alone a newborn. I lived in a tiny closet in my sister's house, babysitting her five children to help pay my way. I barely had a roof over my own head, now I had to find shelter for two. I felt like I was alone. My siblings had their own lives. My dad and stepmother were off limits. Several people told me I could stay with them after my delivery, but no one said that I could live with them. That's a big difference.

The pregnancy was uneventful. But as my delivery date grew closer, my fears about the future grew larger. I delivered an 11-pound, 3-ounce girl—a giant of a baby. She was stillborn.

I sank into a deep depression. Then one day, I had a revelation of God's unconditional love and mercy for me. God knew I was not ready for motherhood. I believe He took my baby to give me an opportunity for a brand new life. This discovery filled me with peace.

People around me were mourning, but I found the strength to console them. "Please don't cry. Please don't be upset," I urged. "This is a wonderful thing. I'm healthy. I'm going to be fine." I focused my thoughts on this second chance to make something of myself. I was determined to make something good happen in my life.

Years later after my daughter, Toya, was born, I just loved her. She was so beautiful, a dream come true. However, I needed to return to work because times were tough. I didn't have money. I couldn't afford to buy baby stuff. Thankfully, my girlfriends and sisters came to the rescue and gave me their children's hand-me-downs. My grandmother would say, "You make do with what you have." That's exactly what I did.

As a baby gift, someone gave me diaper service for 60 days. In my mind, heaven had just opened up. Only wealthy women had diaper service, and here I was, putting hand-me-down baby clothes on my little angel, while setting diapers aside to be picked up by the service. It was magical. What a special gift. The diaper service could be viewed as a metaphor for Toya's birth—wealth and happiness beyond measure.

Clearly, the miracle of Toya's birth is the best experience of my life. And my most defining moment—bar none. It shaped me in ways that I could never imagine. The knowledge that I would be the one to provide for her, guide her and love her was both awesome and humbling. The opportunity to care for another human being is one of life's greatest privileges. Never take it lightly. What a blessing.

## South Africa and Stepping Out of My Comfort Zone

I love learning new things, meeting new people and exploring new places. I was invited to visit South Africa by the nation's government for a community relations initiative. I jumped at the chance. It was in the mid-1980s and South Africa had begun to dismantle apartheid, its system of racist policies. I wanted to speak with everyday South Africans living out this historic moment, and show a side of their country typically overlooked by American news coverage.

Although I had traveled to Europe and the Caribbean, I had never visited Africa. I was eager to soak up everything I could during the 10-day trip with other members of the press. We toured Johannesburg and several other cities and villages. During our stay, South Africa was facing civil unrest. I asked if my group could visit Sun City, an area forbidden to black Americans at that time. I wanted to see what all the fuss was about. "That's up to you," I was told. "Take your chance." Naturally I did, and our group toured Sun City. Some of the journalists, however, did not share my enthusiasm for adventure.

For instance, I went 1,800 feet down into a platinum mine—where you're made to remove all your clothing, watches, jewelry, underwear, everything. You are given a jumpsuit to wear with high boots, a hard hat with a light, and gloves that came up to your elbows. You're completely covered with only your ears and face exposed.

I asked, "Oooh, can I take a little piece of platinum back just to prove that I was really in here?" Of course, I was kidding. Well, half kidding. The answer was a serious no. In fact, no platinum comes out of that mine, except for mining purposes. After the tour, the jumpsuit and gloves went into a vat, and I went into a shower with filtered water. When you enter and exit the mine, nobody touches you, you don't touch anybody. The whole process was explained very sloooowly, as if to say, "Don't try it, sister!"

I really wanted to meet the miners. Word was that they were very abused and misused. Supposedly, they left the mining camps only on Fridays to visit their families, then promptly returned on Sunday evening. It sounded depressing and dehumanizing to me, but that was the way they lived and worked.

The living quarters at the camps were sad. The miners stayed in sparse brick huts with few beds. Some even slept on the floor. Most of the miners didn't like me questioning them about conditions at the mine. They took my concern as an indictment of their alleged mistreatment. The miners did not believe they were victims of exploitation. Compared to other local salaries, they were well paid. And they seemed quite comfortable with their situation. After considering the miners' perspective, I suspended my judgment. Who was I, an outsider, to say that they were abused and misused?

However, I was pleasantly surprised by the South African court system. One of the press tour stops included a visit to a local bar association. I met the area's senior top judge, who invited me to attend a court session. It was fascinating; the docket was so well planned and the efficiency was admirable. In South Africa, when court was scheduled to start at 9 o'clock, it started at 9 on the dot. The design of the courtroom was equally impressive. The bench was shaped like an arc, and the senior judge sat top-center above everyone else. He invited me to sit with him at the top, and I readily accepted.

Most notably, this judge heard 11 cases from start to finish that day. There were no continuations. He listened to all sides, he made his ruling and the decision was swiftly carried out. I remember one guy got 11 years and that was it. He didn't get to go home and say goodbye, but was immediately taken into custody. No appeal.

I left the courtroom utterly impressed with its decorum. Then I saw another side.

I was suddenly awakened in my hotel room very early one morning and told to meet the other journalists in the lobby. We were greeted by government officials, who informed us that student dissidents had blown up the area's electrical utility company equipment. As a result, my plans to speak at a local university were abruptly cancelled.

The officials then issued strict orders: "You will keep your regular schedule. You will not go to the university. You will go nowhere near there. You will stay together. You will be protected. You will be taken care of." We listened quietly like obedient children. "When you come out of your hotel, you will be examined before you get into the van, so do not take anything that you don't want to find on the ground."

I did not understand the reference to the "ground," but I soon learned. When our group left the hotel, we were met by armed members of the military—our so-called protection. I stepped out the door, carrying my purse and a little bag. A tall, uniformed man, clearly in charge, spoke to me in broken English.

*Defining Moments Revisited*

"Drop it on the ground," he ordered. I couldn't understand his thick African accent. "I beg your pardon?" I asked. He did not repeat his words. He took the end of his rifle, lifted my bag from my arm, and dropped it on the ground.

He then took the barrel of his firearm and literally rifled through my scattered belongings. When he finished his search, he finally spoke. "Pick it up." I got his message loud and clear.

South Africa was undoubtedly a life-changing journey. The experience made me extremely grateful to be an American. I thought I understood poverty. But that trip opened my eyes to the abject conditions of developing countries. South Africa also deepened my appreciation of the human spirit. Despite some deplorable surroundings, the South African people were warm, loving and proud. The miners took pride in their work. The judge and attorneys took pride in dispensing justice. I assume the military guards took pride in their positions. They certainly took their duties seriously.

Most significantly, South Africa showed me that I am more than a Chicagoan, more than a United States resident. I am a citizen of the world. We are citizens of the world and we must meet the needs of our global community. Live your life like a tourist. Always discovering new friends, new lessons and new adventures.

# 8

## A Mother's Love

Poets, philosophers, writers, politicians and everyday folks all speak about a mother's love—the special kind of love that knows no bounds and tolerates no obstacles. But what happens when your mother dies at a young age? Who provides that special "mother love" that all children need?

Picture a skinny 12-year-old girl, braids flying as she runs into her family's third-floor apartment. She grins as she proudly holds her report card from Carter Elementary School. She hands the report card to her dad. He smiles brightly as his eyes radiate warmth, care and congratulations. That little girl was me.

Seventh-grade school work did not come easily to me. I had to work extra hard just to earn average grades. This report card was very special. I ran down the hall to show it to my stepmother. I shoved it in her hands and exclaimed, "I got all As and a gold star!"

She interrupted me. "What time is it?" she asked. I could feel my heart pounding. She repeated the question, "What time is it?"

I rambled as I tried to explain my tardiness. "I know I'm late, but Mrs. Robinson asked me to stay just a little bit late after school, because she said she needed help cleaning the classroom. She just needed a little help. I stayed to straighten up the chairs and have that room ready for September, when we return to school. I got to draw on the board, a bowl of fruit with cherries and bananas."

"Give me that report card," she demanded. She took it from my hands and threw it in the china cabinet. "Go to your room," she ordered. I walked slowly, trembling. She followed me. I looked up into her round brown face. I could see the squint of her eyes just before the first blow of her fist landed against my head. The blows kept coming as she beat me about my face, head, arms and chest. She then grabbed my blouse at my throat and slammed me against the bedroom wall.

"I told you, you cannot be late getting home. Two minutes, five minutes, ten minutes. You are not to be late," she said, her face inches from mine, her hot breath in my nostrils. "You are not to disobey me. You will be punished for the summer. You will not leave out of this house for the whole summer. You will go as far as the front porch. You'll look down on the kids playing out there this summer. You will not go out to play with them."

Something came over me that day. I had enough of her. An inner strength, or perhaps it was an inner insanity, pushed words out of my mouth. I blurted out, "You're the meanest person I know. You're just so mean, and God doesn't love you 'cuz He doesn't love people like you. He can't possibly." I revved up, tears running down my face, mucus running out of my nose, and my bruised face and chest throbbing with pain.

I would like to tell you that the skinny 12-year-old triumphed that day. I would like to say that my righteous indignation changed the balance of power between Esther and me. I would like to say that we came to some kind of an understanding after my heartfelt rant, but it never happened.

Staring at me with the coldest of eyes, she pushed the bed closer to the window. She reached into the closet, pulled out a length of rope and tied it to the bed. I didn't fight or try to get away as she calmly tied the other end of that rope around my legs and pushed me out of the third-floor window. I hung upside down by my ankles, dangling three floors over the concrete pavement. Like laundry waiting to dry.

Eventually, an "angel" in the guise of a neighbor saw me hanging upside down from that window and threatened to call the police if she didn't pull me back into the apartment. She pulled me in, spewing profanity at the neighbor and me. That was not the first time I was beaten by her, nor would it be the last.

Today, an incident of child abuse is reported every 10 seconds. But in the late 1940s, when Esther was dangling me out of the back bedroom window, few statistics were kept about child abuse, and even fewer people intervened. Back then, it was one of those dark family secrets that no one discussed. No one came to my rescue. I guess everyone was afraid of her and left me to fend for myself. Of course, there were some caring relatives, teachers and my downstairs neighbor who comforted me and provided a brief respite from the abuse.

Thankfully, other angels appeared at the right time. My fifth-grade teacher, Mrs. Robinson, was one of my life angels. She made such a difference. Her classroom was a refuge for me. A place where I felt safe, loved and connected to the world. A place where I could simply exhale.

On more than one occasion, I confided to Mrs. Robinson that my stepmother had beaten me until I was raw. I said, "Please don't make me sit down. If I could just stand like I'm being punished in the back of the class, it'll be OK." Mrs. Robinson would go along with my requests. Other times I would say, "Could I please sit in front of your desk, but please don't call on me. I know the answers. I have the answers. I wrote them down." I would give her my homework so she knew that I had completed the lessons, but I could not participate in class because my head hurt so badly from Esther's beatings and my spirit was so damaged.

I had been Esther's victim since we moved into her home a few years after my mother died. It was an unusual arrangement. She moved her husband into a back room of the apartment. It was only when I became an adult that I learned she never married Dad.

"The only reason that you're with me is because you are the baby of all the children and there's no place to put you," she told me. My other siblings were old enough to live on their own, leaving behind my brother Alphonse and me. Alphonse could do no wrong. I could do nothing right. "I don't like girls," she told me. "Girls are bad. You're never going to be anything."

My older siblings tried to help me, but they knew that every attempt triggered her to brutally beat me. The best thing they could do was to stay away. For instance, my sister Thyra tried to speak to me while

I was walking home. Of course, Esther beat me. She attacked me anytime I looked happy.

The abuse was more than just physical, it was also emotional and spiritual. From kindergarten until fourth grade, I attended St. Anselm Catholic School. There was an altercation between my stepmother and a nun. Naturally, I was too young to understand the details. She kept me home from school one day. The next day she told me, "You go back to school today and you will walk up to the sister, and you will slap her face as hard as you can."

I was horrified. "I can't. She's a nun. I can't. God will not love me anymore if I do that," I cried. And she said, "You either do it or I'll beat the hell out of you." I believed her. I went to school and slapped the nun in her face, which ended my student career at St. Anselm. I regret that I never got to explain to the nun the reason I slapped her.

I think about not having my mother whenever I hear my good friend Nancy Wilson sing the George Gershwin classic, "Someone To Watch Over Me." The tune speaks to the common hunger for a loving figure in our lives. For the fortunate, the first person who fulfills that role is mother. But because my mother died when I was 2 years old, the hunger for mother love carved a deep chasm in my life.

I remember very little of my mother, Agnes. Her photos and the recollections of my older siblings have helped a bit, but are poor substitutes. That hunger was only intensified by my evil stepmother, who definitely was not "someone to watch over me."

My mother's twin sister, Naomi, remained a constant presence in my life, despite Esther. When my mother died at age 42, Aunt Naomi had made a deathbed promise to look after her sister's children. This was a promise that Aunt Naomi took seriously, even though she lived in New Orleans while we lived in Chicago. She also was afraid of Esther, who decreed that no one, especially extended family members, could have contact with me. They could not talk to me, see me nor send me any gifts.

*A Mother's Love*

One spring day when I was in fifth grade, Aunt Naomi boarded the City of New Orleans train to visit Chicago and me. As I played in the schoolyard during recess, I saw a woman limp her way down the street and thought, "that woman walks like Aunt Naomi." One of my aunt's legs was shorter than the other because of a childhood mishap, giving her a permanent limp. Her signature gait enabled everyone to identify her from blocks away.

As the woman limped closer, I realized that, sure enough, it was Aunt Naomi. I locked eyes with my dear aunt through the schoolyard fence. Too afraid to move as other children played around me—perhaps Esther was watching—I offered Aunt Naomi a small smile. She returned the smile along with a tiny wave. She knew I would get in trouble if I talked to her.

The bell rang signaling the end of recess and all the kids ran back into the school. Aunt Naomi stood watching me outside that gate until I went inside. She then turned and walked back the way she had come. I was alive, in school and healthy enough to play at recess. Aunt Naomi had kept one part of her promise. Satisfied that she saw for herself, she took the train back to New Orleans.

My aunt would make other visits to make sure that I was alive. She taught me the importance of family. Just watching her standing there, watching me, illustrated that family cared. Family is committed. Family shows up. Family comes through. Her smile at that playground fence said it all. That was all she could give me, a smile and a wave. Those simple gestures told me everything about love. I am sure Aunt Naomi was praying for me.

You probably wonder why I didn't run away. I tried, but a series of events forced me to stay until Esther sent me away. One evening when I had more than I could take from her, I told her husband, "I'm going to run away." He was a very nice, quiet man who rarely talked. He went to work, came home and stayed in the back bedroom, emerging only for meals or conversations with my dad. I said, "I don't have any money." He flipped a coin at me, saying, "Well, here. Here's a dime."

In the 1940s, a dime was a fortune; it was real money. I sneaked out, clutching the dime in my hand. I ran over to Indiana Avenue and took a jitney cab to my Aunt Vera's apartment at 37th and South Parkway (now called Dr. Martin Luther King Drive). Vera was my father's sister and lived three blocks from her sister, Anita.

Aunt Vera rented in a building that did not allow children. I went to her window and softly called, "Aunt Vera, Aunt Vera, Aunt Vera" until she hustled me inside. I revealed that I ran away.

"Esther's going to kill you," Vera said. "Oh my God, you shouldn't have come here."

"I can't go back," I insisted. "I'm going to stay here tonight."

Aunt Vera was scared to death of Esther. My aunt believed that she would kill her. Aunt Vera sent me down the street to Aunt Anita, who told me I could spend the night, but I had to return to Esther the next morning.

"If you try to stay away, she'll find you and she'll kill you," Aunt Anita warned. "But if you go back, she'll just beat you, and you'll be fine."

The next morning, Aunt Anita woke me up, gave me cab fare and sent me back. But before I left, she gave me advice on how to survive the wrath of Esther. She told me to ask for her forgiveness. She warned me to hold my tongue even when Esther pushed me to the limit, come home from school on time and do my chores without complaint.

I passed my first-floor neighbor as I climbed the stairs to our apartment. The woman stood so that Esther could not see her talking to me. "You ran away," she dryly said. "You tell her that you are so sorry and that you'll never, never, never do it again." I don't remember her name but she was a very nice lady. Unfortunately, her words could not save me.

I knocked on our apartment door and Esther roughly snatched me in. She forced me down on my knees and beat me so badly that I thought I was dying, but somehow I survived, again. She held me by my braids with one hand and pounded me with her other hand. "Say you'll never do it again," she demanded. Crying, I agreed to never do it again.

Years after I tried to run away, an angel appeared just when I needed her. She walked up to me at the local grocery store and asked, "What are you doing with all those groceries as big as you are?" I was married and pregnant with my daughter and near my delivery date, but my husband and I had to eat, so I had to go shopping.

The woman, who I later called Momma Inez, continued to question me. "Who's going to carry all of those groceries? You can't carry all of that," she declared, snatching the bags from my hands. Inez walked me to my apartment, put away the food and peppered me with more questions—when was the baby due, what did my husband do, was I a Gabeau? I wondered how she knew I had elements of Louisiana Creole in my blood.

*A Mother's Love*

Her next question cemented her place in my life.

"Where is your mother?" I replied that I don't have one. In her no-nonsense fashion, Inez declared, "Well, you got one now. I'm coming back to see about you." And she did.

I learned a lot from Momma Inez. She played a key role in helping me become the woman and mother I am today. She had a style and humor that enabled her to attract three husbands and the good will of everyone she met. She mothered me in a way that was needed, when it was needed. Inez believed I could survive and thrive. I learned through her that I was not destined to repeat the cycle of abuse with my daughter. That it is my choice to be the kind of mother I want to be. If it is to be, it is up to me.

I promised never to raise my hand against my daughter. But once I fell short of my goal. Toya wanted to go with her friends on an outing. When I told her she could not go, my obstinate 8-year-old child picked up a large pair of scissors and hurled them at the picture window in our apartment. The toss did not break the window, but instead broke the tips of the scissors. "How dare she throw scissors in this house!" I thought. "Because she didn't get what she wanted? Really! Who was this willful child standing in front of me?" I was shocked. Almost with a mind of its own, my right hand flew up and slapped her across the face.

Those few seconds of ensuing silence seemed to last an eternity. I couldn't believe that I had slapped my child, the kid that I loved dearly. My child, who had never been slapped or hit, couldn't believe it either. As the red imprints of my fingers rose on her cheeks, she began to wail and so did I. Who was crying loudest my daughter or me? That's a question that I can't answer, even today.

I apologized for slapping her and promised never to do that again. In my best Momma-tone-of-voice,

I calmly discussed her behavior. As we talked, Toya cried—not from the pain of a blow—but for disappointing me and for being so rude and disrespectful. Our conversation ended with hugs and kisses.

That emotional experience with Toya showed me how easy it is to resort to physical punishment to discipline children. Sometimes even the best-behaved kid can pluck the last nerve of the most loving parent. Of course, that does not justify beating children. Rather, I hope it helps you recognize anyone can succumb to the temptation, especially when stress strikes.

*A Mother's Love*

The scissor incident occurred when I was a young, single mother. Over the years, I have developed an acute awareness and sensitivity to the mistreatment of children and women. I turned the pain and bitterness of my battered childhood into action and advocacy. As a broadcaster with WGN-TV and spokesperson for various child abuse prevention organizations, I have strived to educate the public on the plight of the abused and neglected, and inspire people to help these children.

In my private life, I practice what I preach. I have nurtured many young people who needed it. I cared for several youngsters in my home as their informal foster parent. Those arrangements usually were short term and ended when the parents' situation improved.

I also helped college students pay their tuition, even financed the full four years to keep promising young adults from dropping out of school. Those young people will always hold a special place in my life. One, in particular, holds a special place in my heart.

When Richard Wright reached out to me, I was a young, single mother and a radio personality on WBEE Radio. He was about 14-years-old, living with an aunt and uncle because his mother and father had died. Richard's father died when he was about 7 and his mother was killed when Richard was about 13. Although Richard was not physically abused, he was living in a less-than-ideal situation. His aunt and uncle had their own children and financial issues to manage. Richard simply wanted someone to give him that special mother love that all children need.

I remember that young man sitting in the waiting room of the radio station. The receptionist told me he had been waiting to see me for some time. I escorted him into the studio with me, assuming he was interested in a broadcast career. "I heard you on the radio and I like your voice, and I like you," Richard revealed. "I don't have a mother or father. Would you be my mother?" He asked just like that, straightforward. At first, I thought he was joking, but looking into his face, I saw the seriousness of his request. I explained that I was already a single mother with a daughter, then added, "But I'm willing to be your friend."

From that point on, Richard and I became like family. I attended his high school, undergrad and law school graduations. I watched him grow into a productive adult. He became an attorney and is now a minister. Eventually, I legally adopted Richard as my son. The formal adoption was not about inheritance or any other legal issue. I wanted Richard to know he will forever be part of my life. I am very proud of him.

Often, reporters and others will ask me about the most important achievement of my life. They are referring to some career highpoint, of which there have been many. But without a doubt, unequivocally and undeniably, the greatest success of my life is my daughter, Toya. Our relationship is so very special. We are girlfriends, but we are mother and daughter first.

My primary role is mother. That's critical for today's parents to understand. Parenting means understanding that we are human, we will make mistakes and we will stumble in this journey. As adults, we must apologize for our mistakes, forgive ourselves and others, and work to do better next time.

Parenting can come from many sources. You don't need to be blood to be family. If you did not receive the parenting that you needed growing up, seek it from others. It's that important.

If you were blessed with good mothering, consider sharing some of that mother love with others. This does not have to be a formal foster care or adoptive relationship. Spend time with a young, single mother to help her develop that special bond with her children. Show her loving ways to communicate and discipline her children.

Remember, children are God's everyday miracles. The next time you hear the classic melody, "Someone To Watch Over Me," hopefully you'll understand that all children—no matter their age or stage—need someone to watch over them. That someone could be you.

# 9
## *Everyday Miracles*

Thank you, Father. Thank you so much. Thank you for the gift of another day. Please surprise me, because I need a miracle today. Maybe I need two or three miracles. They don't have to be big ones, since you know what I need. Thank you for all that I have.

Before I even open my eyes, those words come rushing to the front of my mind. We have so much to be grateful for—every one of us. No matter what challenges you're facing, no matter how bad you think things are, if you are reading this, if you are awake and alive, God has smiled on you. He has given you the miracle of another day. Your very life is a miracle.

Miracles are all around us. In the summer of 1974, Illinois started a statewide lottery and being the first official host, I was the public face of the lottery. It was a great responsibility. Every day, before going on the air I would pray, "Dear Lord, please let somebody win. Let somebody win who really needs this money."

Occasionally, I would pray to let somebody I know win the money. One day both of my prayers were answered. Greg, an office intern in his mid-20s, won more than $20 million in the Illinois Lottery. His family really needed the money. He was the primary support of an aging mother and a younger sister. All three were living in a tiny North Side apartment that was designed for one. Unfortunately, Greg died about seven years after winning the money. I don't know what eventually happened with his family, but while Greg was alive, he put the money to good use and made sure that his family members' lives improved.

My early years with the Illinois Lottery were simply amazing. Every winner was a miracle to me. Whether walking down Michigan Avenue or at a fundraiser, it would not be unusual for someone to run up to me and say, "You pulled my number and I won $5,000." The money seemed like a gift from heaven to the winners. Winning the lottery for thousands or even millions of dollars can seem like a major miracle. Most people were genuinely grateful.

To really make your life something special, it's important to be grateful for every day, every mundane miracle. My morning prayer is actually my waking ritual. I invite you to create something similar for your waking moments.

When we wake up, we typically replay a movie in our heads full of "gotta," "shoulda" or "coulda." I "gotta" get the kids up. I "gotta" get ready for work. I "shoulda" gotten gas for the car yesterday. Before we recognize what a glorious moment each morning is, each rising is, we have already closed our minds to the gratitude of ordinary things. I would like you to make your first waking thoughts, "Thank you, thank you, thank you."

I regularly ask God to surprise me, and does He ever. Every day there are obligations, duties and requests that I don't think about on rising. We all have them. Those responsibilities are written down on my to-do list. Yet as I'm brushing my teeth and getting dressed for the day, it hits me like a thunderbolt of inspiration—the answer to whatever quandary was present. Surprises like those only happen when you're able to trust in God, trust that He has your best interest at heart, trust that His surprises are just what you need and trust that He will send miracles your way. Most of those miracles are ordinary, mundane ones. Miracles that are easy to overlook or ignore.

My attitude about gratitude did not just happen during my adult years. Gratitude was part of my belief system even as a young child. We always said our blessings before meals, and we were taught to say

*Everyday Miracles*

"thank you" and "please." It instilled a basic sense of gratitude in us. I also understand the reality of want. For instance, to be able to put a dime in the basket at church was a moment of gratitude. I knew that some kids didn't have a dime to give, so they would put in a nickel. Some kids put in a penny and some didn't have anything to give to the church. There were Sundays when I was one of the youngsters who didn't even have a penny to give. I would watch the basket pass me by. That was a sad moment. I was extremely grateful on those occasions when I could put a dime in the basket.

Even my wedding when I was in my early 20s was certainly a miracle—a direct result of knowing how to make money go further than anyone thought it could, especially my then-fiancé's mother, Hazel. A socialite in the African-American community, Hazel didn't think very much of me. My family had little social standing and even less money. I certainly wasn't a woman of loose morals or wild ways. Still, I was not her first choice for her son. In Hazel's circle of friends, the wedding had to possess certain amenities worthy of her standing in the community.

At that time, I was working for several attorneys in an office near 47th and South Park (now King Drive). One day, a client who owned a detective agency overheard a conversation about my pitiful wedding. "I heard your future mother-in-law say that you didn't have any family background, and talk about your wedding plans," the client said. "I'm going to show her. I'm giving you $1,000. Can you get a dress and plan a wedding for that kind of money?"

Back then, $1,000 could have been $1 million. Not only could I plan a wedding for a thousand, but if I added the money I already had saved, I could throw a real society shindig. I did.

For years afterward, Hazel questioned me about how I got the money to plan that type of wedding. My only response to her was that I saved for it. My frequent response to God was thank you.

Many times just what you need shows up just when you need it. That's a hard-won lesson in trust and gratitude. The appreciation for hard lessons did not come easily for me. I don't think that they come easily for anyone. Still, when we are given a situation to face, there is a lesson in the making. It's on each of us to determine the lesson to be learned. Those lessons represent our own unique test, created and designed just for us. We must learn to be grateful for the less-than-pleasant events as well as the life-changing ones, like winning the lottery.

Our lives are full of miracles—small blessings and over-the-top, heart-stopping wonders. No one questions that surviving a kidnapping and shooting is a major miracle. Surely appreciate the mega-miracles when they arrive, but it's the mundane miracles, the ones that might appear as ordinary events or even challenges, that I hope you recognize.

Believe in miracles and be grateful for them. Share in the awesome gift of gratitude. Borrow a page from Chicago-style politics—when you say thank you, say it early and often.

# 10

## Find Your Dance

I love to get on a dance floor and move to the rhythm of the music—slow or fast, with or without a partner, mostly in private. Dancing is just an awesomely powerful experience. I enjoy the freedom it offers. The way I can just let myself go. When I need to boost my energy, I dance. But when I need to boost my spirit, I get quiet and dream big. My life is filled with high hopes, big dreams and quiet, prayerful moments. All of that gives my life balance.

Several years after my kidnapping and shooting, I attended a Dental Society Dance with a good friend who was a dentist. I had a ball. I rarely left the dance floor. I finally paused to catch my breath and chatted with two other male friends. They seized the moment to satisfy some of their curiosity about me, although they couched it as a medical concern since they were doctors.

One asked, "We all wonder did you ever get any psychological help?" The other one chimed right in, "Because you're always so effervescent, you're so nice to everybody. If you didn't get some help, how did you do that without any therapy?"

Basically, they were asking why wasn't I crazy? The kidnapping and shooting could have—should have—left me emotionally broken. I was not offended by their questions. It's only natural to wonder how I survived the ordeal with my sanity intact. I explained that I did not seek therapy and I try to be nice to most people. The conversation was intense, yet sincere.

As we talked, a dentist approached and asked me to dance. I politely declined his invitation, then added, "We're in a deep conversation here." His response stunned everyone.

"God, I hope you're not talking about that thing that happened to you," he said. "You need to get over that." His timing could not have been worse. He made the comment during a break in the music, so several people heard it. Before I could respond, my two friends simultaneously confronted him. The anger in their eyes was plain. Noticing the abrupt change in everyone's body language, my date ran to my side, puzzled. "What happened?" he asked. "What did you do? What did he do?" I laughed, grabbed my date by the hand and hit the dance floor. The DJ had started playing one of my favorite songs.

When people say something thoughtless or outrageous, go to wonder. Wonder why they would say such a thing? Wonder what's wrong with them? Wonder if they are three dancers short of a chorus line. When that man insulted me, I had a choice to make. I could have gotten angry. How dare he tell me to "get over" such a life-changing event! Would he have gotten over being kidnapped, shot twice and left for dead? I could have let his insensitive remarks hurt me, or I could laugh off the entire episode, wish the dentist well and keep on dancing.

Sadly, there's not enough dancing or hope in many lives today, especially young lives. I think about the troubled young people I meet and their tragic stories. Many are so smart. Many are kids who just have no idea how intelligent they really are. As often as I can, I talk to these young men and women. More than talk, I listen. I hear the hopelessness in their voices. I see it in their eyes. Their quiet despair, their secret longing for a different life, their unrealized potential shouts louder than their boasts of bravado. It breaks my heart.

Gun violence has escalated. Children are raising children. Parents have decided to be friends with their children, rather than major decision makers in their lives. The influx of drugs has taken parents out of the home and placed them in jail, wrecking the family structure. Now, you have grandparents rearing their grandchildren on their Social Security income. The economy also plays a major role in crime. There are few jobs for uneducated young adults and families are losing their homes due to foreclosure. Though there are some visible efforts underway, our educational system is not committing enough resources to prepare students for America's strong future. The cutbacks in school music and arts programs are leaving too many of our youth with nothing to do.

I recall an anti-violence conference I attended at the Hilton Hotel in Chicago. Some of the young participants were gang members. Others were students whose lives had been touched by violence. One young man revealed that he was preparing to graduate from law school. Law school? I was baffled. I asked him, "What are you going to do? What do you expect for the future?" he replied, "I'm going to represent my people." His "people" were fellow gang members who needed legal representation. "I know what to do. I know what to say. I know how both sides think," he asserted.

Even though this young man never spoke of renouncing his gang affiliation, he was so sure of himself, so confident about his abilities and his plans. The key difference between that future attorney/gang

I am at age 3, riding my new red
cle through Washington Park in
ago.

My beautiful mother, Agnes.

My handsome and dapper dad, J

My grandparents, Nanny and
Pappy—Emily and John.

Aunt Naomi, my mother's identical twin sister.

Family time: That's me at the far left with my siblings
Doris, Ernest, Thyra, Alphonse and Dad.

Aunt Vera, my sisters Thrya, Doris and me.

Personal time walking with my granddad.

Three generations of girls
(clockwise, l) Toya, Marissa and me.
(Jennifer Girard Photography)

My husband, Nick, and I at our
wedding reception.

"Merri Dee the Honeybee," as was called, hosting "The Mer Dee Show" on WBEE Radi with special guest Samm Davis Jr. (right).

Making history as the first black female commentator at the Chicago Auto Show in 1964. This began my broadcast career.

Backstage with my best friend, legendary songstylist Nancy Wilson.

Making dreams come true as the "Lottery Lady" on WGN-TV with Ray Rayner, the late host of "The Ray Rayner Show."

Enjoying a moment with the late Chicago Mayor Harold Washington and his assistants, Kari Moe and my daughter, Toya Campbell.

Congressman William (Bill) Gray, then-CEO of UNCF, and I at annual fundraiser. I helped to raise more than $100 million for the UNCF, one of my favorite charities for more than 30 years.
(Dot Ward Photography)

Chatting with Lou Rawls and Quincy Jones in L.A.

My greatest passion remains encouraging children to dream big.

Sharing my philosophy, "If it is to be, it is up to me."

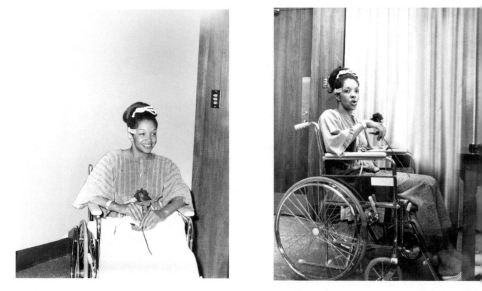

At press conference as I am being released from the hospital after bein
kidnapped and shot twice in the head in July 1971. It was a miracle that
survived. I am forever grateful for God's grace and mercy.

An insightful 1971 interview with actor Peter Graves on finding a cure for cancer.

Attending a Black History Month salute with Illinois Secretary of State Jesse White and jazz legend and longtime friend, Ramsey Lewis.

Backstage with Stevie Wonder during a star-studded UNCF gala at the Kodak Theatre in L.A.

Presenting an award to legendary author Dr. Maya Angelou.

Quincy Jones always makes me laugh. I was touched when he surprised me with an autographed copy of his book, "Q: The Autobiography of Quincy Jones." He wrote: "To dearly beloved Merri Dee, I feel so blessed to know you…May you live as long as you want and never want as long as you live. I love you. I celebrate you. I will cherish our friendship always."

Celebrating with two cool gents, Smokey Robinson and Chicago radio legend Herb Kent, at a gala in Chicago.

At city event with former Chicago Mayor Richard Daley. (Antonio Dickey Photography)

Only Nancy Wilson could have surprised me with the UNCF Lifetime Achievement Award in 2007. (Victor Powell Photography)

Talk show host Phil Donahl in Chicago.

Striking a pose with media mogul Oprah Winfrey at a fundraiser.

...eting Barack Obama in
...cago's Washington Park
...he nationally televised
...Billiken Parade. We both
...icipated in the annual
...de festivities. (Jerome
...nons Photography)

Through the years.

(Jennifer Girard Photography)

member and the typical gang member—hope.

Once we change how we view gang members, we can alter how we address their desire for respect and responsibility, perhaps by replacing some of our communication and resources with education and personal attention. When someone believes in you, you believe in yourself better. Perhaps with better vision and attitudes, we can help them hope and dance in their hearts again.

Seeing young people as gifts of life, seeing them as better than they see themselves is something I've been passionate about for some time. Back in the 1970s, I reported on sports for WGN-TV. At the time, the most that I knew about games like basketball, football or hockey was that they were played with balls, except hockey, which was played with a stick and a puck. To get better informed for my job, I visited several playgrounds across the city and also went to a few high schools and local colleges to see kids play. Frankly, I didn't get a lot from those experiences, except that one coach said, "You're from Channel 9? You have to come back and see these kids play."

So I went to that particular game and the players were all over the court. Back and forth, up and down, shooting across the court, hitting the basket. It was as if they were jet-powered. Those little jets ended up

*Find Your Dance*

being Mark Aguirre and Terry Cummings. I also saw Isaiah Thomas, Doc Rivers, Tony Brown and Darrell Walker play. They were absolutely fantastic at playing basketball, but their grades? A few of them not so great. They were all about playing and not as interested in the books. I thought about ways I could help them use the game, and not have basketball use them.

Sometime later, Bob Love, who then was a starting forward for the Chicago Bulls, and several other professional players were at my home for lunch. Between filling bowls with steaming gumbo, breaking open crab claws and slurping out the crabmeat, the discussion turned to young players. Thinking about Aguirre, Cummings and the rest, I blurted out, "I want to start a boys' basketball foundation. I don't know anything about doing this, but I think we need it."

One word led to the other and a foundation was born called Athletes For Better Education. Bob Love, Chick Sherrer (who played at Princeton and was the college roommate of Sen. Bill Bradley) and I were the founding members. The foundation offered a summer camp and after-school program for promising players. It included academic study with a curriculum developed by several college professors. We provided the students with intense basketball practice after school, and kept them involved with English and math classes on Saturdays. We included such topics as money management, dining etiquette and speaking skills. Once this was up and running, I started a mothers' club. I would meet with the moms while the students were in class. You bet those mothers made sure their students were present on Saturday mornings.

Someone once asked me, "Why do you want to do this? You don't even have a kid in any of this. You got a girl, she's not playing ball." I responded, "You're absolutely right, but these children are our children, and they need us. We need them educated because if they keep on progressing the way they are, they're going to make it to the NBA. They'll represent us in Chicago and across the country. God forbid if they can't read, can't write or don't know how to speak in front of a camera." That was my impetus.

People just kind of went along with me. At one point, I was speaking with the mayor about the foundation. The question came, "So what do you want?" My reply was, "$50,000." I got that $50,000, matched from someone else, and the foundation was born.

Those six students went on to have careers in the NBA. They played well and became coaches. I take great pride in that. I'm still in touch with a few of them. For instance, I was walking through O'Hare Airport in Chicago and I heard a male voice

*Find Your Dance*

call out, "Hi, Mom." I have a daughter, so I knew this voice couldn't be directed to me. I turned and saw that it was Doc Rivers, who is one of the "winningest" coaches out here today.

I've always had a special gift to see the best in someone. Sometimes they don't see it themselves. Great teachers can recognize potential. I don't call it some mystical thing, just a gift to see beneath one's surface. That is what our teachers see, great potential in our children.

You must find some time to hear your heart song. What will it take to make your heart sing or dance? Your heart knows the answer. It knows how to obtain it. You just have to envision it, listen to it, believe in it and work at it.

# 11

## Loving And Accepting Yourself

When I walked across the high school graduation stage, I could honestly say that I had survived and accomplished more than some predicted. I knew my life would be just fine.

An unfortunate early pregnancy was part of my life journey, but even that experience didn't diminish my belief that my life would turn out well anyway. My baby was stillborn, but I believe that in a way, even that was a gift to both of us. I wasn't ready to be a wife or a parent. God knew what was best.

I remember my 20s as an exciting time in my life. I wanted to do everything. I wanted to travel. I wanted to have a good job that paid well and enabled me to help my family. I wanted it all.

Some believe that my amazing career was foretold. My mother-in-law from my first marriage, Hazel Dorham, read tarot cards for fun. This prim and proper Chicago South Side socialite with a keen business sense would sit in her living room laying out the cards—and my future plans.

"You are going to do something in radio," she predicted. "You are going to move on, my poor son." It was as if she just knew that I was going to leave my husband and her son, Sonny. My response was to laugh heartily. Working in radio never entered my mind prior to Hazel's prophesy, but the thought apparently stuck. Later during my Midwestern School of Broadcasting days, her words would return, even though I was determined to go into radio engineering.

Still, Hazel and I had a rocky relationship over social status. Over time, she became more of a mother than I expected. I learned a lot from her. I learned about accepting myself despite what others thought. She taught me about society life, and how not to be afraid of it simply because I was unfamiliar with its rituals and traditions. She showed me how to fit in with anyone and everyone. If I didn't feel comfortable, she explained that I was more than equal to anyone in that "special crowd."

Later, I learned that Hazel based her sense of superiority on a false premise. Her first husband, her son's father, had spent several years in prison. That was information Hazel kept hidden from her social circle, and from me. Her snootiness evaporated after

I learned her family secret. My family background wasn't so bad, after all.

In many ways, she pushed me toward self-acceptance by showing that everyone, even the society people, had hidden blemishes and scars. Those were important lessons—lessons I share with others. By the time she died, we had become good friends.

You are good enough, smart enough, strong enough and pretty and handsome enough, despite what others might think. Not to say that you shouldn't work on self-improvement, but do it for yourself, not because someone disparages or belittles you.

*Loving And Accepting Yourself*

Accept that you are blessed, that you are held in the palm of God's mighty hands. No matter your circumstances, you always have something to share. Giving brings healing to you and to those you serve. Try it.

You never know how helping someone in need will end up changing your life. Consider my friend, the Rev. Dr. Willie Wilson. For this humble man, a life change represents a life charge. I met Willie about 25 years ago when he called my home at 6 a.m. because he wanted to be on television. Who doesn't? To this day, I don't know how he got my private telephone number. Instead of getting angry at this stranger for waking me so early, I was very pleasant. For some reason unknown even to me, I listened to him and decided to help.

Through the years, I have come to appreciate his drive and self-acceptance. His early life was as difficult as mine. Willie grew up dirt-poor, working in the cotton fields of Mississippi. As a youth, he spent a few years in prison. He eventually overcame his troubled past and became a multimillionaire businessman, philanthropist, gospel singer, television producer, minister and doctor of divinity. He has owned several McDonald's franchises and started four very successful companies. Not content to rest on his success, he helps others change the direction of their lives. He gives so much money from his own pocket to worthy causes that he rivals my fundraising efforts.

If you ask Dr. Wilson how he accomplished so much, he gives credit to God and to the many people who have helped him along the way. He takes little credit for himself. His life story proves that turning tragedy into triumph is possible. Not only for a lucky few, but for anyone and everyone, even you.

Here are six measures to guide you on the path to self-love and self-acceptance:

1. **Embrace change:** You are not your history. If there is something you don't like, change it. You can change

the situation or you can change the way you feel about it. Either way, change is the critical action to take.

2. **Dump regrets:** Whatever happened in your life has brought you to where you are now. Focus on the present and the future. If you are responsible for past mistakes, make amends to those you have wronged. Forgive yourself and move on. Avoid wallowing in the past.

3. **Appreciate your resources:** Even if financial resources are not plentiful, you have other valuable resources. Do you have an inquisitive and insightful mind? Are your friends loyal and generous? Count your many blessings. Write them down in a daily journal.

*Loving And Accepting Yourself*

4. **Know your worth:** You are smart enough, strong enough and good enough to deserve a great life. Own what you are good at, accept it and share it. Be creative.

5. **Give back to your community:** To those much is given, much is expected. Share your time, talents or treasures with others.

6. **Live with an attitude of cautious fearlessness:** Do something that is challenging and new. Develop a fresh skill. Live on your own. Find your dream job. Seek new love. Embrace your commitment to your family. No matter how hard, go for it. Even if you don't succeed, realize that failure is no indicator of

your worth. Failure is not final.

Every action you take to move forward can strengthen your confidence and resolve to love and accept yourself. Live abundantly in your mind, it just may manifest in real life.

# 12

## Forever Friends

I have enjoyed great friendships in my life: Andrew, MaryJo, Dottie and Monika, but one in particular comes to mind. As a child growing up on Chicago's South Side, Alyse Jones proved her friendship several times over. She was a fearless protector. When others would tease me or hurl insults my way, Alyse defended me.

When I didn't have any money to buy candy after school, she shared with me. "Here, Mary Frances, eat this candy bar," she would always say. "Don't take it home because you'll get in trouble. You know how your stepmother is."

I always appreciated her friendship as a child, but it wasn't until later that I really understood the depth of that bond. When we graduated from eighth grade, we were bound for different destinies. As 12-year-olds we didn't truly understand what that meant, except that Alyse was to attend a neighborhood high school, while I was being sent to school in New Orleans. We may not have understood the different destinies, but we did understand the 900-mile difference between us.

One of the things she said during that period was, "If anything ever happens to you, you can always come back to my house because my mother will let you stay here." She went on, "Besides, she's always liked you, so I know she'll help you." Even today, I wonder why she offered me the shelter of her home. How could either of us have known that one day I would take her up on that offer?

My stepmother decided that two years at St. Mary's Academy in New Orleans was enough. She wasn't going to pay any more tuition for me, which meant that I had to leave. When the nuns took me to the Greyhound bus station and put me on the bus, I didn't know who would pick me up in Chicago. After reading the letter from my stepmother, I didn't know where I would live once I was back in the city.

Somewhere along the route, I recalled Alyse's words. When I arrived in Chicago, I called her mother. True to my friend's words, she allowed me to stay with them. Like the women of that time, one of the first things she said to me when I arrived at her door was,

"Are you hungry? Have you eaten?" Such a welcoming sentiment, so unlike the one from my stepmother when I called to speak with my father. The gist of her conversation was, "You'll do fine. Let us know where you are." There was no interest in helping out or anything. I stayed with the Jones family for a short time and I've never forgotten the friendship even though our lives went in totally different directions.

That's the thing about friendships. Real ones can be based on common interests and needs, or nothing in common. That's why it is so difficult to tell the difference between friends and acquaintances. During my childhood, my father often said: "In order to have a friend you must be a friend, but you're OK if you don't have a lot of friends. As you grow up, you won't have a lot of friends. You may have a lot of acquaintances, but friends will be few, so cherish them."

*Forever Friends*

Choice is an important element of friendship. You can't choose your family, but you can choose your friends. You do the choosing and do not wait to be chosen. It's all about self-esteem and making wise choices about the kind of people who deserve your friendship.

I have been blessed in choosing good friends and good acquaintances. My friendship with Jann Honore grew over time from a professional association with the United Negro College Fund (UNCF). What started as two women joined together to raise money for college-bound students blossomed into a valuable relationship. We share confidences, good times and hard truths. We can laugh and cry with each other.

She was there when I made a very public blunder that was very embarrassing. It was the 2004 UNCF Scholarship Award dinner in New York City. The then-UNCF President Bill Gray, a former U.S. congressman, was presenting scholarships to outstanding African-American students. To my surprise, I was presented the organization's highest award. Bill began to talk about my support of the organization and offered some very gracious remarks about me. I was almost speechless, but not quite.

I thanked everyone for their support of the UNCF and expressed my appreciation to JPMorgan Chase and Target for their special donation in my name. I acknowledged the love and support of my family, particularly my husband. "Before I sit down, I'd like to recognize a person in the audience that has been so important in my life, my husband, Nicholas. He doesn't like it when I do this, but he's just a true Trojan in my life." The audience chuckled. Not sure what was so funny, I continued, "Well, he is, and I think everybody needs protection."

The entire audience erupted with belly laughs. I remained clueless as to the reason, until Jann told me afterward, "Did you realize that was almost like a condom commercial?" I was so embarrassed. New York was one of the first cities to run condom commercials. Like a true friend, Jann helped me to see the hilarity of the situation. We still talk about that event and laugh.

Through the years, I've lost good friends like Michelle Clark, a CBS-TV reporter investigating the Watergate scandal in Washington, D.C. On her return flight to Chicago, the plane crashed, killing most of the passengers and several on the ground. I had been at WGN-TV only a few months when news of the crash came through the newsroom. There was speculation that Michelle had obtained information that would have made the Watergate cover-up even more of a national scandal.

We were going to have dinner that night. Instead, I was ordered to be on camera immediately to report on the crash. Back then, reporters read the manifest (the names of the passengers). When I came to her name, I could not say it. I was too emotional and teary. The camera cut away, thank goodness.

While Michelle and I were colleagues, we were also friends. I was more concerned about the death of a truly special friend than of a gifted investigative reporter. We have to keep our priorities straight.

Following that broadcast, Fahey Flynn, a much more seasoned and well-respected newscaster from another station, said he was very impressed with me. He saw my heart and told me I should never lose that sensitivity.

I've learned that friendships may come and go, but having a relationship with God lasts forever.

Even as a child, I would sit in church and gaze at the altar asking for a pat on the head, to show that He loved me. I wanted and needed His protection, because many times I felt that no one would save me from harm. As I grew older and continued to seek guidance, my faith became stronger and stronger. I realized that I was loved and would always be protected. I had a special friend. This kind of relationship is a powerful gift to share with anyone, especially our youth.

Real friendships can span a lifetime. After I lived with the family of my childhood friend, Alyse, we drifted apart. I often wondered what happened to her.

I found out about her while recovering in the hospital after surgery. I woke up and saw a young woman cleaning the room. She was taking a long time. I was in a lot of post-operative pain and just wanted to be left alone. Thinking that she was on the medical staff, I said, "I don't want any pain medicine, I want to go home." We both knew that I wasn't going anywhere, anytime soon. I fell back to sleep.

When I opened my eyes sometime later, she was still there and introduced herself. "My mother was your best friend when you were younger and you lived at her house," she said. I immediately knew she was talking about my buddy, Alyse.

She recalled how Alyse always told everyone that she knew me growing up. She joked that Alyse called me by my given name, Mary Frances, and always said that my "stepmother was crazy." She told me her mother had recently died and had been buried about two weeks before my hospital stay.

I asked, "Why didn't she contact me? Why didn't she find me or call me or something?" She explained, "My mother was a very proud woman. She just loved the idea that she could just look at you on TV, know that you were good friends and that you were OK. That was as much as she needed."

To the very end, Alyse proved to be a great friend—one who delighted in my accomplishments, but didn't want to use our friendship for her own gain. She had my back in my youth and later. I will always treasure her.

Finally, you need to be your own best friend. That means being good to yourself before taking care of anyone else. It also means saying thank you the moment you wake up and then taking a minute or some time specifically for you. You are your first responsibility. That's why flight attendants instruct passengers to put their oxygen masks on first before assisting others. If you don't take care of yourself, you cannot take care of others.

# 13

## When I Think Of You

I was dressed in a suit that the love of my life enjoyed seeing me wear. It was green and black, very stylish and elegant. Walking with my head held high, but my heart heavily burdened, I found a seat near the front. I had come to pay my respects, to bury the man I loved.

Several people, including a few of his close friends, his sisters and their husbands, didn't want me at the funeral. I attended anyway. My presence was not about protocol, etiquette or their wishes. My presence was about the relationship between the two of us.

Sitting there—alone in a crowd of his family, friends and business associates—I couldn't help but think back to the first time we met. Divorced with a young daughter and little money, I needed to find work to support us. Several close friends suggested that I try modeling. I signed with the Shirley Hamilton and the Playboy Modeling agencies and was hired to model at the Chicago Auto Show in 1964, becoming the first African-American to showcase new cars.

At the show, a balding, slightly pudgy gentleman introduced himself to me and struck up a conversation. He had a warm smile, an engaging sense of humor and a courtly manner, unlike many of the other men I had known. Even though he was about 15 years my senior, I was soon taken by him. By the end of the weeklong show, he asked me to dinner. I agreed and scheduled the date for a week later. I later learned that he was a prominent businessman and the owner of several auto dealerships.

So many memories came back as I sat there at his funeral. Some made me smile amidst my tears. We were together almost 15 years. He helped me rear my daughter and was a father figure who adored her. Even now, she occasionally brings up a small incident or event that the three of us shared. She keeps his legacy and love alive by talking about him. My family thought very highly of him. My sisters and brothers welcomed him into their homes. He became a member of our family.

As much as we enjoyed our years together, there were times of deep sadness. I was with him when his

9-year-old son died. We had planned to leave town for a weekend when we received a call from the housekeeper that his son had taken a bad fall and needed surgery. We rushed to the hospital to be with him. When the doctors operated they discovered that his little body was riddled with cancer cells. The end came quickly. We were heartbroken. I helped him get through the overpowering rage and bottomless despair that comes with burying a child.

He often talked about getting divorced and wanted us to get married and have a child together. Though I love kids and love being around them, I had Toya and didn't want any more children.

*When I Think Of You*

Truth be told, I didn't want to get married again. I didn't see any reason for it. We had everything we needed: a 10-room house in the city and a 14-room house in the country. My daughter was in private school and I had a great, well-paying position. He had provided for his children very well. After dealing with my stepmother and my first husband, I promised myself never to be dependent on anyone again.

I understood that our relationship affected his whole family. While we initially were very discreet, he eventually became very open about our relationship. It's hard to keep that kind of secret, even in a big city like Chicago.

Holidays were never easy for him. I think he missed us more during those times. While he spent time with his family on the actual holidays, he always made sure he celebrated with us either before or after. For me, the situation was different. I had family nearby that I could always visit and my daughter and I also had our own holiday traditions. Since I was a radio personality who often worked on holidays, the arrangement fit right into my schedule. I was grateful.

When he became ill and was hospitalized, we still talked every day. I would visit him in the hospital during the evenings, after my shift had ended at the TV station. I would spend most of the night at his bedside. However, it got to the point when he did not want me to visit because he did not want me to see him in his decline.

Seeing my love in his final repose forced me to remember the day he died. My daughter and I went to the hospital to celebrate her 21st birthday. We arrived with cake and balloons to bring him some cheer and acknowledge his role in our lives. When we arrived at the hospital, he was already gone. I met him when my child was about 7½ years old and he died on her 21st birthday.

I owe him so much. He helped me secure corporate

sponsorships for my radio and TV shows in my first year. That was major for an on-air personality to bring sponsorship to a station.

He taught me the business of media. "You are in a charming, celebrity business but don't forget this is a business," he always said. "Someone is always making money. Make sure you handle business like business."

He believed that I had the talent and drive to make it in broadcast. He was in my corner when I got my first radio show on WBEE in 1966.

While he certainly enriched my life, Toya and I also brought great joy to his life. We enjoyed a loving relationship based on mutual trust and respect. We were always there for him. I know he knew that.

He was a sensitive and liberal man who once served as the president of the Chicago Urban League and created many opportunities for people in the arts. As I think back about him, I recall the major financial leadership role he played in the founding of Little City Foundation, a lovely facility for children and adults with disabilities in Palatine, Illinois. I became a frequent volunteer at the foundation. The experience enriched my life. What a kind, thoughtful man he was.

Our big issue was race. He was Jewish and I was black during the height of racial tension in the 1960s. It was a big deal to see a white man with a black woman or a black man with a white woman. There was a lot of pressure on any interracial couple during that time. Not many dared go out in public and do the little ordinary things that lovers enjoy, like shopping, dining or going to see a play. But we did. We felt we deserved it.

He and I were not married on paper, but we were certainly married in our hearts. Would I do it again? I would like to say no. It brings hurt and heartbreak to both sides. I don't want to hurt people and I don't want to hurt either. I have learned that you should never say never. If you live long enough you may find there are no easy answers. Life is not always that plain and simple. There is a gray area not easily explained. Still, I try to do unto others as I would have them do unto me.

My first marriage to Walter "Sonny" Dorham when I was 19 lasted about seven years, but there were problems from the very beginning. After the first year, I realized it was a loveless relationship on both our parts. Yet, he wanted to have a baby. I did, too, just not with him or in this marriage. Eventually, I gave in, became pregnant and had a lovely child who has always been such a blessing in my life.

My husband worked for a dress company and

would bring home the most beautiful clothes for me to wear. He had great style and knew all about fabrics, texture, lines and proportions. He knew what would look good on me. His mother told him I did not spend enough money on my wardrobe.

To make extra money he got involved with guys who were running numbers. This was the illegal precursor to the state-run lottery system. It's kind of ironic that years later, I would be the first host to touch the numbers for the Illinois Lottery. His business kept him out all night. Sometimes he wouldn't make it home until six o'clock in the morning. Basically, we didn't have a marriage or even a partnership because he was never around. I did everything myself—working, managing the home and taking care of our little girl. Like many mothers, my life revolved around my child. My husband didn't have a place in my life and that was fine with him.

One day an IBM job recruiter that I had met asked me, "Do you think you would like to go to school and learn about computers?" My answer was, "Absolutely. How much does it pay?" He went on, "Well, there's travel involved." That fact rocked me a bit. I didn't think I could take a job that involved travel. Not to be deterred, the recruiter said, "Ask your husband. Talk to him about it. The job pays $700 a week." Seven hundred dollars a week! That was a king's ransom in the early 1960s. The recruiter might as well have said, "We'll pay you a million dollars."

A couple of days later, I mentioned the job to my husband. "Um, I was offered a job," I nervously said. "But it means that I have to travel." The words came out in a rush. I filled him in on the details. I would work in the local office for two weeks and then travel around the country possibly for one to two weeks. I had already talked to one of my sisters about keeping the baby. The entire plan had been worked out by the time I talked to Sonny.

He sat there and didn't say a word. After a long pause, he finally asked, "You really would like to do this?" I told him yes. He said, "Go ahead and do it." No questions, no comments.

I later discovered his true motive for agreeing to my IBM job offer. With me on the road, he didn't have to report to anyone and didn't even have to come home, and he could share in the wealth of my income. I suspected that he was fooling around.

One time when I came home unexpectedly, a woman was in my house with him. I didn't say anything. I didn't make a scene. Instead, I simply turned around and left.

On another occasion, after some snooping, I discovered that he was dating a young woman who lived on our block. One day when he came in, I said, "You know what you need to do? You need to marry her."

He looked at me, all wide-eyed and innocent and said, "Marry who? I'm married. I'm married to you."

I replied, "No, you need to marry the lady that you're sneaking around with because you're not married here. This is not a marriage and it's time for us to stop fooling each other. So here's what I suggest. Get married to her. I'll give you a divorce. Very easily, very quickly. I don't want anything from you, and you can't get anything from me."

Our marriage was in such a bad state that the thought of him cheating didn't bother me. My plan was to work, put money away and get ready for the day when I would leave.

Little did I know that there were several lessons in store for me before I could execute my strategy. First among them was safeguarding my earnings. True to my plan, I saved as much money as I could. But as I was socking away money for my big move, he was raiding our joint savings account, buying furniture and other items for his girlfriends.

*When I Think Of You*

When I tried to make a withdrawal from our account, it was practically empty. He had taken the money I had earned. That was a hard and costly lesson, but one I learned well.

The final straw came on the evening I treated my sister Thyra to dinner and the musical, "My Fair Lady." I had just returned from a weeklong business trip and wanted to thank her for her support. After the final curtain call, I told her, "I'm not going back." She asked, "Do you mean backstage? Who do you know in the play?" I explained, "I don't know anybody backstage. I'm not going back home. I'm unhappy. Sonny is unhappy. It's time to move on." I remember the sad, confused look on her face as she exclaimed, "No one in the family has ever divorced!" That was significant for we had southern, Catholic roots.

Toya and I moved into a hotel for a few days while I made more permanent living arrangements. True to my word, I didn't go home that evening and never lived with him again. I left everything. I didn't even take a toothbrush. I did take bluesman B.B. King's advice to never make your move too soon. Trust me, I didn't make my move too soon. I made it right on time.

It took 34 years for me to get married again, but when I did—whew! What a blessing.

Yes, I dated several people in between that time. Some of those experiences were pleasant enough. Others either ended quickly or limped along in relationship purgatory until they ended. I was no longer a good "dater." And I certainly wasn't looking to get married. I wasn't opposed to the institution, but I didn't need it. Every marriage should have its own mix of need, want and desire. None of my relationships had all three. The good ones perhaps had one, occasionally two; others only one or none.

In many respects, this was an issue of trust. I wanted to trust men, after all, I had been in a solid and trusting relationship with the love of my life. I had also been around and seen much of the world, which helped me understand that trust was precious—something to be protected and not squandered.

My faith in God was important, so if a man belittled that faith or refused to recognize it, there was no room in my life for him. There were others who wanted to be with me, but did not want to include my daughter. That definitely was not going to work at all. It was also quite puzzling because at that time, Toya was 23 or 24 years old. She was not a child, so it wasn't as if a kid was going to get in the way. Then there were the guys, because my daughter and I were roommates, who fantasized about having both of us. A couple of

*When I Think Of You*

them were even bold enough to say it. Needless to say, those men didn't even get their phone calls returned.

It became clear that dating was not enjoyable and I didn't really need to do it. I had much more fun going out with my girlfriends or platonic male friends. So for a long time I didn't date.

That is, until Toya was preparing to get married. As the mother of the bride, I had a million things to do and plan before her wedding. Nicholas Fulop, the head of the University of Chicago's private Quadrangle Club, was the person who would help me plan the reception. He was slated to help pull off my only daughter's wedding, which had to be perfect.

At one of the early meetings, we had a slight disagreement. He tried to explain that what I envisioned was not the proper way to hold a wedding and reception. Finally, I said, "Sir, I know that you've done a lot of weddings. I've discussed this with my daughter and her future husband and they have placed this initiative in my hands. I know what I want and this is how it is going to be." With that said, I gave him my set of rules, regulations and protocols.

Nicholas still laughs about the meeting. "I had done 3,000 weddings before," he says, "and I had never run into a mother who knew exactly what she wanted. Exactly." We worked together and the wedding turned out spectacularly.

It was during the period between the planning and the wedding that Nicholas asked me on a date. "I could just date you and only you," he said. There's something about courtly and courteous men that I find very appealing. He seemed absolutely comfortable in his skin. His Old World European ways, his integrity, his honesty and sense of self inspired much admiration on my part. There was another element that was intriguing. When we met, I was a well-known Chicago personality, having been on WGN-TV for around 20 years. I had anchored the news and sports, served as the station's editorial spokesperson, hosted the daily lottery and many TV specials. Yet he had no idea who I was. What a delightful and refreshing change.

*When I Think Of You*

I had a lot to learn about him, too. Like his experiences living in Communist Hungary, escaping and returning to search for his parents. He found them and spirited them out of the country. I was fascinated by his dedication and determination. "I was a soldier in the United States Army," he proudly said. "That is where I received all of my opportunities for education and to be an American."

Nicholas made sure that I knew he really liked me. By this time, I really liked me, too. It took some time and some living for that to happen, but it did, and I was happy. I had grown to like me. I knew how to be still within my own skin.

We had been together comfortably for several years when Nicholas informed me of his plans to retire and move from his home on the university's grounds. "I'll have to find a place to live," he said. "You can come live with me," immediately popped out my mouth. As he has demonstrated time and time again, his primary thought was about my welfare. "Oh my God, I couldn't do that," he said. "What would people think of you?"

That's when I knew, this is it. This is it! Nick was the right man for me at this stage of my life. I didn't need a man to pay my bills or provide for me. I needed a man to be honest with me. Nick is. I needed him to have integrity and to have my back. No question.

The next day, he turned to me and asked, "Why don't we just get married?" I answered, "Fine." But I was thinking to myself, "Are you crazy, Merri? You're going to have to give up all your freedom. He's not like your friends. Hell, he doesn't like many of them. He doesn't fit in." I thought all sorts of things. However, the strongest, most calming voice came from my baby girl and best friend, who simply said, "You better marry him; he's a catch Mom." That sealed the deal.

A few of my concerns were valid. I had tremendous freedom in how I lived and I was very accustomed to coming and going as I pleased. I had no intention of changing at this time in my life. So before we took our vows, I asked Nicholas if he could deal with my lifestyle. His "yes" came much too quickly. So I bluntly asked, "What does my freedom mean to you and how will you deal with it?" That started a good, clean and deep conversation that lasted several days. Nicholas was prepared to give himself over to whatever I wanted. I was happy and honored to be given such a gift, the gift of his heart. I had to make sure that he could handle all that I had become.

That candid conversation made sure that our marriage was built on a foundation of honesty and integrity, just like Nicholas. Of course, we had to make other accommodations for each other. But those adjustments, like finding a condo to accommodate Hunter, our 110-pound "puppy," were minor in the grand scheme of things.

I got married at this time in my life because I wanted a companion. Finding men to spend time with me was never a real problem. I had boyfriends and even platonic male friends. Finding men with whom I wanted to spend time was more of a challenge. I was selective and wise in choosing men. And yet, I also understood that if my experience turned out to be a fling, well, I could do that too. But that certainly would not be my choice.

Did I finally discover need, want and desire with Nicholas? The answer is obvious. Yes!

I've always known that I have a lot to offer, so much to bring to any relationship. I can be fun, loving, generous and challenging—all the things that people want in life. You too have so much to offer, so much to bring to any relationship. I ask that you never sell yourself short or cheaply. Don't put yourself on the dating discount rack.

Romantic love starts with loving yourself. Once you have a deep and abiding love affair with the person in the mirror, once you feel safe in your relationship with your Maker, then you won't feel such a desperate ache to have a man or woman in your life. Concentrate on what you do have. Do you have young people in your life whom you love? Then show them. Do you have a skill or hobby that brings you satisfaction? Then find a way to share that talent with someone. What other blessings now fill your life? Be grateful, then share yourself with someone special.

Sometimes the best way to find romance is to stop looking for it. Instead of searching for your soul mate, focus on all the other things you want. Be clear about your goals and vision. Understand the difference between love and lust. Remember, being alone is not the same as being lonely.

You are worthy of the best. Find your love song. Follow your heart, but only give it to someone who you truly believe deserves it.

*When I Think Of You*

# 14

## Everywhere You Go, There You Are

There are no coincidences in life. Everything happens by design. What has happened was supposed to happen. Yet, you are the captain of your fate, the master of your soul. You have the power to chart the course of your life.

I believe in destiny, fate and seizing control of your life. Our lives are guided by what is supposed to happen, the energy of the universe and by the decisions we make or don't make. Many of us fail to observe the cycles and seasons of our lives. When we take the time to do so, the realization of such reflection can hit like a Mike Tyson punch. We're doing the same things, going through the same motions, reliving similar events and expecting a different outcome. That's not a healthy process and it just does not work.

Doing the same things over and over can hurt our hearts. Your heart speaks to you. It knows what you really want and understands you better than anyone. Some describe this voice as your inner voice, the voice of the universe or the voice of God. Others call it your gut feeling when something is either very right or very wrong. No matter how you describe it, this voice wants what is best for you. It has your best interest at heart. I urge you to listen; this is a powerful voice.

This is the voice that will tell you, "No, you're not crazy; yes, your world is askew." It's the inner feeling that says you seem to be making the same decisions in similar circumstances. It points out the life lessons that must be learned. Rest assured as in any school, there will be tests and quizzes. The frustrating thing is that invariably life gives you the test first, then the lesson. Too often, the most crucial lessons come from difficult experiences. It's one of those puzzles of life. Most pleasant experiences don't teach as much or as well as the more painful ones.

I've said it before, it's not what happens to you that matters. It's how you respond to what happens that matters most. When something unpleasant happens, it's wise to ask yourself, "What's the lesson I'm supposed to learn?" And follow up with, "What's the opportunity here?" The answers to both will move you beyond surviving life's trials and tribulations to succeeding against the odds.

Everywhere you go, there you are. It doesn't matter how much the external conditions change, until you deal with yourself—the person in the mirror—you'll experience the world through the same eyes.

Coincidences seem to crop up in my life. While I was a student at St. Mary's in New Orleans, one of my best friends was a girl named Angela. She and I simply clicked as good friends. Angela was a day student, which meant that she went home every day after school, while I was a boarding student. Angela and I shared secrets and giggled together as young girls do. We always shared stories about her mean grandmother and my mean stepmother. We would regale each other with tales from home, trying to outdo each other with outrageous anecdotes about the heartless women in our lives.

Years later as an adult, I returned to the school and convent. I actually had fond memories of the place. It became a place of refuge, a place away from my stepmother's hell. I also wanted to find my childhood friend, Angela. We lost touch when I left after my sophomore year. To my delight, the nuns remembered us and gave me her contact information.

We later reunited. Seeing her after all those years was indeed special. She remained unchanged; the same warm brown eyes and the same mischievous smile. Our bond had survived the passage of time. We giggled, laughed and shared stories about our lives as if we had just seen each other yesterday.

It was during this visit that I asked about her "mean old grandmother." I suspected that by then, her grandmother had died. She described her grandmother's heart attack while climbing the steps to her apartment after returning from church, how she lingered for several weeks before dying and how only a few family members attended the private services.

In all the stories we had shared about her grandmother, never once did I ask her name. "Was your grandmother's name Esther?" I asked. She took a moment to answer, and gave me a puzzled look instead. When she finally answered, I already knew the answer: Angela's mean grandmother and my cruel stepmother were the same person. Amazing!

Coincidence? I know there are no accidents. There was my stepmother in my life, again. Only this time, instead of destructive vines that tethered me to despair, she was the link to one of my best childhood memories. Something good came out of my relationship with her—a lifelong connection with her granddaughter. Someone who knew and understood the pain she had caused me and others.

When I think about the trauma of the kidnapping and shooting, I realize that part of my life's purpose was to survive that experience both physically and emotionally. I survived the snide remarks from some colleagues in the media who said things like, "I wonder what really happened?" I also survived the vicious gossip in the African-American community that maybe this happened because I had once dated a white man. Most importantly, I survived the insensitivity of the criminal justice system when my assailant was given a light prison sentence. Again, it's not what happens to you, but your response that matters. I endured all of that and even more, because I was not alone. The love of my family and friends sheltered and protected me. Love brings healing power. I am so blessed!

And what was I supposed to learn as a result of the kidnapping and shooting? It proved that I was stronger than I initially believed. I was a survivor. It also gave me my life's mission. I was kept here to help others, of that I am certain. My purpose was to advocate for victims of violence. I also knew I should keep my heart open for the opportunity to nurture and encourage others.

*Everywhere You Go, There You Are*

What is the purpose of your life? You have this book in your hands for a reason. Either you selected it or someone cared enough to give it to you as encouragement. There are incidents but no accidents. There's something in these pages that you are meant to read; there's something in your life that you are meant to review.

You are not destined to live in uncertainty, despair or disappointment. You are supposed to live with purpose, clarity and joy. When you concentrate on clarity of self, you can honestly say everywhere I go, there I am—as the master of your fate and captain of your soul.

# 15

## If He Hits You Once...

I lived a lie. Like so many women, I held onto a secret. A secret so deep that I dared not share it with my closest friends. I was a victim of domestic violence. My then-boyfriend slapped and shoved me during our on-again, off-again relationship.

In all of my motivational speeches to women across the country, I never talked about it until now in this book. Domestic violence did not fit the brand name that I had built for myself. People expected so much more from me. What would they say if they knew what was going on behind closed doors?

My physically and verbally abusive beau was a popular R&B singer who rose to the top of the charts in the early 1960s. I thought I might have found someone special. But like so many women, I ignored the signs. As Dr. Maya Angelou says, "If someone shows you who they are, believe them." I think the old adage says it best: "If he hits you once, he will hit you again." There is never just one time; there is always one more slap, one more shove, one more hit. It never stops. I am a witness.

I will never forget the big fight. It was soon after my 1971 kidnapping and shooting. I found a gun in the drawer of my bedroom dresser. As you can imagine, I was frightened and angry. I trembled when I saw that gun. I didn't want to touch it. I just wanted it out of my house. After all that I had been through, the last thing I expected to see was a gun in my house. I called him and told him, "This has to be yours. Come and get it out of my house right now!" I screamed.

The moment he walked through the door all hell broke loose. He was angry because I had yelled at him on the phone. His attitude was, "You are my woman and I can do anything I want." He pushed me and I fell on the floor. He picked me up, shoved me and said, "I am not going to hit you in your face." I guess he was smart enough to realize that if he struck my face, people would automatically know that he abused me.

Shocked and defiant, I hit him back. I pushed him with all my might. I was shocked at myself for fighting back. He towered over me, he won. I remember my dad's words when I was little with my brothers: "If you raise your hand to a man, expect to get up off the floor." I was fighting for survival. My teenage daughter saw everything and called the police. "Go on and call the police," he taunted me. "They are not going to believe you."

Ladies, what happened next might surprise you. Two cops came to my door and my boyfriend let them inside and talked to them in the hallway. He told them I was fighting him. That was indeed true. Yes, I was fighting him—fighting for my life. They arrested me for hitting him! What? A man hits a woman and the woman is taken to jail? Here I am, battered, bruised and disheveled, being hauled off to the Chicago Police Headquarters and locked up.

Remember, it was a different time period. Back in the 1970s, men stuck together. Cops often sided with the men and made the women feel like we deserved to be hit; we started it. Women did not report abuse or even rape because the cops often would not believe them. Men would always win.

I posted bail and got out of jail very early the next morning. I quietly had my record expunged months later. Fortunately, the Chicago media did not learn of the incident. I did not want my supervisors at work to know. I feared that if word got out, my livelihood would be jeopardized. He knew that and held that over me and threatened to embarrass me publicly.

That was the last time he hit me. I finally got the strength to dismiss him. I had forgiven him before, but not this time. I was freeing myself. No more lies or excuses.

It's been said that people who were abused as children often grow up to become abused adults or abusers themselves. During our time together, I made excuses for his abuse. I never should have done that. I was abusing myself by staying in that relationship.

I am always impressed when someone speaks up and tells the truth about abuse. Years ago, I met a woman who was not afraid to give a voice to the voiceless women. Linda Fay Walls candidly details her abuse in the book, "Surviving Heartbreak Valley" (Strategic Book Group). She reveals that she was hit, held at gunpoint and raped, and even saw her four children burned to death in a house fire set by their father.

I urge women to look at those early signs of a potential abuser. There is information there. Knowledge is power. If he has a short temper, he might take it out on you. Choose wisely. Don't think just because he looks dapper in a designer suit, that he is a catch.

Looks can be deceiving.

If you find yourself in an abusive relationship, get help from the police, family, friends, your church or a community organization. Stand tall and don't blame yourself. Don't be ashamed or you will stay where you are, the way you are. Remember, this is about you, all about you. Take responsibility for yourself and get help. No one can help you if you don't speak up and speak out.

# 16

## Gifts From God

"C'mon guys, stop playing with the lights," I said with a humorous lilt to my voice during the commercial break. I thought the WGN radio crew was playing a prank on me by dimming the lights.

I had to deliver a 60-second live commercial during a taped show and my sight had dropped to the point that I could hardly read the words on the two sheets I held. One of the engineers quickly answered, "Nobody touched the lights in the studio, what are you talking about?"

It seemed as if I had fallen into a deep dark hole. I immediately remembered the words of a doctor years earlier after losing sight from the shooting. He said, "You may experience some sight loss when you are older."

Was that what was going on? Was I going blind?

Determined to carry on, I somehow made it through the one-minute read. My sight came back just a little bit more. No one knew—neither the crew nor the two visitors sitting in the booth—I had temporarily lost most of my sight while on the air.

Ordinary miracles can be easily ignored or taken for granted until they are lost. Vision is an overlooked and undervalued miracle. Scientists maintain that the ability to perceive depth, color, distance, shape, form, detail and all the other components of eyesight represents a spectacular evolutionary advance. I say it is an amazing gift that we receive every day upon awakening.

Too often, we blindly rush through our days oblivious to life's more subtle treasures. We fail to appreciate the golden brilliance of the sunrise or the fiery glow of a sunset. The cool breeze on a blazing afternoon, a warm embrace on a chilly night. The fragrance of a fresh rose, the sound of silky jazz and sweet laughter, the lusciousness of dark chocolate. When you awoke this morning, did you open your eyes in gratitude, eager to greet the day? Thankful to see another dawn?

As I shared earlier, I awaken every morning saying thank you for the gift of another day. Truly, each day and every moment are gifts. How we treat those moments are our gifts of thanks to God.

The loss of my eyesight during a broadcast was not the only time that I've had to put a smile on my face and keep moving forward. I don't know any other way to be. Ever since I was a teenager, I've had to cope with head pain due to, I believe, the many times that I was beaten on the head as a child. Those headaches were exacerbated by the bullet that remains.

When people see me at public events, they may not realize that I'm working through pain. My head often feels like it's in a vise, but I press on until I can't.

That happened on the day I was scheduled to move into a wonderful place with a view of the lake. Instead of unpacking boxes in my new home, I endured a six-hour spinal surgery. That was not what I originally planned to do on that day.

Several weeks before the surgery, I had been suffering from severe knee pain. It had gotten so bad that I needed help entering and exiting a car. I thought the pain was arthritis, but it was something far worse.

"What is this in your head?" the doctor asked after reviewing my X-rays and exams. I answered, "I don't know." I didn't even think of the shooting, it had been such a long time ago. Then he asked, "Did you ever get hit in the head?" Of course the answer was yes, a lot, when I was a girl. The doctor explained that I might need brain surgery. I simply wasn't feeling that.

*Gifts From God*

No one was operating on my head. But the pain in my head, my knees and along my legs was so intense. I could barely function, could barely lift my legs or even think.

The doctor made some suggestions to ease the pain temporarily, so that I could think more clearly about his recommendation. In other words, so that I would agree to the surgery. Fat chance. I wondered what other options were available. "I'm getting ready to move into a new home. I have to go to work. I have all these appointments. I promised these people that I'd appear at their events," I explained, citing every imaginable excuse to avoid surgery. "Maybe one or two days," he said. "That's all the time you'll get before the pain intensifies."

Within two days I was in the hospital. The problem was not some mysterious growth in my brain. It was the metal coating of the bullet that remained in my head. The bullet's coating had leaked into my system, damaging muscle tone, affecting the back of my neck and spine. I had the spinal surgery, which helped ease the pain, and I moved into my new home about two months later than planned. I was like a brand new person.

Again, it all makes me appreciate minor and major miracles. With appreciation comes hope.

I have heard hope described as positive imagination. Hope creates a picture in your mind of your dreams fulfilled, your desires granted. Faith focuses your eyes on that mental picture. You see yourself as successful, loved, healed and happy. Belief in miracles brings dreams to life.

All miracles—the grand and the ordinary—are gifts from the Divine. When you appreciate the miracles that surround you, you will see even more of them. The more miracles you see, the more hope you will feel. It's an ongoing cycle that never ends.

*Gifts From God*

# 17

## Giving Back By Paying Forward

Perhaps it was the words of my grandfather ringing in my ears, "What are you going to do for this world?" Or maybe it was coming face-to-face with the presence of the Divine after I was shot when I discovered my life's purpose is to help others. I realized that giving back by paying forward is a major priority.

As director of community relations for WGN-TV and spokesperson for many charities, I have raised more than $100 million for dozens of worthy causes, including the National Committee to Prevent Child Abuse, the Kidney Foundation, the Cancer Foundation, Easter Seals and the United Negro College Fund (UNCF). Some of those millions came from people who told me they didn't have a nickel to spare. I asked for that nickel with a straight face, and they gave it to me because they understood this fundamental truth—when you give to others, you also give to yourself.

When you offer your heart and hands to help when you can, you open your life to receive awaiting bounty. I don't mean to imply that giving is a spiritual barter and exchange. I want you to give from your heart because compassionate sharing is good for you. As Dr. Maya Angelou says, "When you give cheerfully and accept gratefully, everyone is blessed."

If you want to live a good life in a positive world filled with compassionate people, then give generously. Show compassion. Think positively. Be the change you seek. I know this from experience.

Having raised millions of dollars for college-bound students, I know first hand the joy of the human spirit that gives generously. I learned that the average telethon donor was a woman in her mid-40s with two to three kids. She worked to support her kids with the dream that they would attend college. Her modest donation—an average of $25 to $50—is an investment in this dream.

Because of those women and donors like them, I have handed out checks for $50,000 upward for college scholarships. I have met dedicated people who passionately supported the UNCF. One teacher in the Chicago area donated $6,000 to $8,000 every year—on a teacher's salary. A group of educators in Chicago's south suburbs pooled their fundraising efforts. Their initial $7,000 contribution increased to nearly $1 million annually.

How gratifying it is to watch a young person walk across the stage to receive a check for his or her education and say, "Thank you so much for this. I don't know how I would get to college without this donation." It always gives me goose bumps.

*Giving Back By Paying Forward*

I want you to turn your gaze away from your problems and toward others. There are people and organizations that need you. Share who you are and what you have. I've been blessed beyond measure. While it's good to be blessed, it's even better to bless others. Focus on what you can give. Dr. Maya Angelou once said, "I've learned that you shouldn't go through life with a catcher's mitt on both hands. You need to be able to throw something back."

Service to others can be an honor that can occur when you least expect it. Somehow, some way, my name (along with about 24 others from across the country) was included in the Pentagon's Black History Month celebration. I had not sought out the invitation, and to my knowledge, few at the U.S. Army headquarters even knew my name. Yet, here I was, visiting the Pentagon as a priority class citizen for the first time. It was so surreal.

I also visited Arlington Cemetery where I was asked to lay the wreath at the Tomb of the Unknown Soldier. I could not hold back the tears. What a privilege, what an honor. It was one of the highest honors of my life.

About a month later, I was invited back to the Pentagon and asked to serve as a U.S. Army Ambassador. I jumped at the opportunity, after all, I come from an Army service family. My father was a proud World War II veteran and all of my brothers also served in the U.S. Army. The position required that I represent the Army in the most dignified manner with grace, respect and honor. Those are the values the Army holds close. That's how I've always tried to live my life. It was a natural match.

It has been a privilege to work on so many issues. Despite my best efforts, though, sometimes I get down in the dumps. Recently, while cleaning a closet and coming across a variety of plaques and certificates, I wondered, "Have I done enough? What's been the result? Did I make a difference? What more needs to be done? What more can I do."

The world needs you. Find a worthy cause, then

share your time, talents and treasures.

As Dr. Martin Luther King, Jr. eloquently said: "Everybody can be great. Because anybody can serve. You don't have to have a college degree to serve. You don't have to make your subject and your verb agree to serve.... You don't have to know the second theory of thermodynamics in physics to serve. You only need a heart full of grace. A soul generated by love."

*Giving Back By Paying Forward*

# 18

## Power Of Forgiveness

Lately, I've been thinking a lot about forgiveness. My father told me many times, "Forgive those who've done you wrong, because if you don't, they sleep with you." These people will steal your sleep. They will poison your waking thoughts. Until you forgive them, these tormentors will keep you a prisoner of the past.

Revisiting the events of my life has exposed raw feelings that I believed were buried and long forgotten. The constant fear at the hands of my stepmother. The grief over my stillborn child. The terror after I was shot and left for dead. The hostility toward my abusive celebrity boyfriend. Despite my best efforts to purge those bitter demons, they can return to torment me. Still, I continue to forgive.

I have learned to forgive myself for my potentially self-destructive behavior. Yes, I once experimented with drugs. My celebrity boyfriend who beat me and slapped me around also introduced me to drugs after the shooting and kidnapping. I now realize the drugs helped to dull the awful memory of that night. They blocked out the dreadful image of Samuel Drew pointing that gun at me.

In those days, few African-Americans sought therapy to overcome trauma. I certainly didn't and no one suggested it. People believed I had it all together and did not need professional counseling.

Before my romance with the crooner, I rarely drank socially and did not smoke. The more control he exerted, the more I realized that the situation was unbearable. I did not want nor deserve that kind of lifestyle.

I eventually forgave myself for putting up with the physical and verbal abuse. After much thought, prayer and time, I found the mercy to forgive him. I know that he must have been a miserable man to hit a woman and abuse drugs. I wondered what his childhood was like.

The truth is, I was one of the lucky ones. I did get away from him and I didn't get caught up in the drug scene. I woke up one day and said "no more." I stopped it and never went back. I connected to what God wanted for me, what I wanted for myself. I forgave myself for being so weak and vulnerable, and for not seeking the counseling that I desperately needed.

"If it is to be, it is up to me." Those 10 little words summed up what I had to do. Stop blaming others for my choices. "If it is to be, it is up to me."

Sometimes forgiveness requires a power larger than you. I really had to let go and let God. The first few times you try can be difficult. But every time you let go, it becomes a little easier to seize control of your thoughts and bend them to His will. It takes practice but it is possible to let it go.

*Power Of Forgiveness*

I am often asked how I feel about Samuel Drew, the man who shot me and left me for dead. Shortly after the incident, people said things like, "You must be so angry with him." I would reply, "I am not angry with him. I am not." This realization came almost immediately after the shooting. I was not angry with him. I forgave him. I felt sad and sorry for his mother. I heard that she was in the hospital having surgery at the time of the shooting. She had to be crazed with worry and regret. Her son had killed one person and shot another. As a mother, I could only imagine how people were reacting to her; probably as if she had pulled the trigger.

I even forgave my stepmother. But that was

one of the most difficult things I had to do. She tormented me and made my childhood a living hell. She cast me out of the family home at 12 and made me fend for myself at 14. From the time I was 3 until 14, she was the main antagonist in the tragedy that was my life. Admittedly, I retained so much anger toward her that forgiveness was practically impossible.

While coming home from an afternoon church service, she had a heart attack and fell down the stairs of the apartment building where the family lived. The prognosis was that she would soon die. One of her last wishes was to see me and ask for forgiveness. She asked my dad's sister Vera to summon me to her bedside. Aunt Vera pleaded with me to visit her. I declined the invitation several times. She eventually visited my job and begged me to see Esther.

I hated her so much at that point. All I could say was, "Why do I need to go see her? I haven't seen her in years." Aunt Vera cried and pleaded, "She's asking for you. You must forgive her. Remember, that is what you must do. You must forgive her. Go see her." I gave in. My aunt and I went together.

I entered the bedroom and saw my dad sitting in a chair next to Esther. She was propped up on pillows in her bed. Her pallor was gray and her gray hair hung lank and lifeless around her round face. I noticed my mother's rocking chair in a corner of the room. As I went to sit in Mom's chair, she asked, "Would you come and sit over here by me?"

"No," I said, "I want to sit in this chair." I sat in Mom's chair, adamantly rocking back and forth. She told me she was very sorry she had been so mean to me. She wanted my forgiveness.

"Just forgive me," she pleaded.

I sat quietly for a minute. Then I spoke. I made her remember some of the horrible things that she had done to me, like hitting me in my face with her fist for coming home two minutes late from school, landing a broomstick or a razor strap across my back and locking me in a closet with no dinner. I described how she hung me by my ankles out of the third floor window, how she told me I was too stupid to be anything, how she made me stop reading at night with the flashlight under the covers, because I would never be smart enough to comprehend anything.

I reminded her about those things in a flat, dispassionate voice because I wanted her to know that I had remembered everything. I wanted her to know that I had become this fine, wonderful woman, despite her treatment.

Finally, I said: "Under no circumstances am I ready

to forgive you. I hate you. I hope one day to be able to really forgive you. Not for you or anybody else, but for me."

After saying my piece, I stood and walked to the bedroom door. As I was leaving, I heard my aunt crying softly while Dad sat stoically. No one said anything.

She died very shortly afterward. One of her final directives was that my siblings and I would be informed of her death after the funeral services. Even then, her evil abounded.

It wasn't long after her death that I really worked at forgiving her and myself for the hardness of my heart. I prayed for my heart to be softened. My prayers were answered because God just lifted her away from me and allowed me to see her sadness, her anger and her loneliness. I saw a miserable shell of a person who probably had a horrible childhood filled with verbal and physical abuse. That's probably all she knew.

Her cruelty taught me that I didn't want to be cruel. But she taught me how to clean a house from top to bottom. A righteous life skill that's lacking in some people. You better believe I'm punctual. She taught me thriftiness. I can shop with $5 in my pocket and make it seem like I had $100.

Since we're dealing with the issue of forgiveness, it

only makes sense to question the actions of my father, given the harshness of my childhood. After all, my mother was deceased, my siblings were scattered all over and the neighbors were afraid of Esther. Where was my dad when she mistreated me? More importantly, why didn't he protect me?

The situation with my dad, Esther and me was very complicated from the start. Shortly after we moved in with her and her husband, my dad had one of many heart attacks, leaving him frail and weak. He was in no position to complain about too much. He was dependent on her for practically everything. In many ways, he was as much a domestic violence survivor as I was. The difference was she beat me physically, while she beat Dad emotionally and verbally.

It's funny, I didn't know until I was an adult that she and my dad were not married. How could they? Her husband lived there too. I must admit I still do not understand that relationship.

One of the saddest parts of this situation is that Dad and I never discussed what had happened. Definitely not while we were in the midst of her abuse, and we never spoke of it even after her death. I believe that he felt badly about everything, especially because he couldn't or didn't protect me. He probably felt guilty for bringing this woman into our family.

My dad was of a generation that refused to speak openly about painful circumstances, so I never heard his side of events. Still I was very angry with him and went through a lot of changes with him. Of course, I forgave my dad. That's what children do, even if takes them 40 years. Thank goodness it didn't take me that long because I wanted to forgive him; however, it took its own time.

Forgiveness is not easy or painless. Too many people walk around holding onto the bitterness and anger that their mistreatment has engendered. They respond by continually hurting themselves and others. They talk about the hurt as if it happened yesterday.

As important as it is to "forgive those who've done you wrong," as Dad would say, it's more important to forgive yourself. Make peace with your decisions, even the poorly made ones. Too often, we hate and ridicule ourselves for our mistakes, then wonder why the world treats us as it does.

President Barack Obama spoke of forgiveness at the Martin Luther King, Jr. Memorial Dedication on the National Mall in 2011. Dr. King, he said, "understood that to bring about true and lasting change, there must be the possibility of reconciliation." That's what forgiveness is truly about—bringing about true and lasting change. A change of heart. A change of spirit. A change of memory and a change of awareness. Forgiveness allows you to change yourself, your view of your tormentor and your perspective of the event.

Start by forgiving yourself. The power of forgiveness changes lives. Let it change yours. Every night before you go to bed, take a look at yourself in the mirror. Look deeply into your eyes, smile at the reflection staring back and repeat to yourself: "I forgive you. You are doing the best that you can. You deserve forgiveness. You are worthy of this life's bounty. You are forgiven."

*Power Of Forgiveness*

Don't let yesterday's pain and mistakes block your blessings. You deserve the best that life has to offer.

# 19

## Finding Your Path

Writing this book has been a labor of love, a trial of memory and a belief in hope. It has tested me in ways I did not expect. The pain of remembering has brought tears of clarity and sometimes joy. It has truly allowed me to reaffirm my love for life, for family and friendship. My dedication to excellence is firm. My faith is unshakable.

My life has been an emotional roller coaster, full of high-flying thrills and stomach-churning chills. My intent in sharing this journey was to illustrate how one person can transform hardships into opportunities, tragedy into triumph. The ability to do so rests on so much more than luck or good fortune. It depends on faith, courage, attitude, discipline and, of course, God's grace.

Some aspects of my life have been open to public view; others more circumspect. Because I am a media personality, many read about the kidnapping and shooting, but few knew about my bouts with domestic violence. As a supporter of organizations that helped children, many may have heard about the abuse of my childhood, but may have missed my excitement as I advocated for children waiting to be adopted into a loving home.

You have a duty to live the best life that you can because so many people depend upon your success in order to achieve their own. That's as true for you as it is for me, and it's the reason this book was written: to motivate others to change their lives.

**Stuff happens:** In your life, there are two events over which you have no control—the day you are born and the day you die. What's in between is yours to fill with gratitude or despair. I invite you to fill it with gratitude because it doesn't really matter what happens to you, what truly matters is how you respond to what happens. Some of those days will be heart-pounding moments. Deal with it, because stuff happens.

**Define yourself:** Know who you are, what you want and what you are worth. Getting this information may require spending moments of reflection, meditation and research. Imagine what your life will be like when your goal is achieved. Visualize how your life will change. See yourself doing whatever it takes to reach this goal. Define yourself and own the definition!

**Be grateful:** Count your blessings. Many happy people do this on a regular basis. Consider writing down your blessings in a journal for later review. Be sure to appreciate both the extraordinary and ordinary miracles that occur every day. When you are presented with a challenging situation, rest assured there's a lesson in the making. And those lessons represent a customized, specially designed course—just for you.

*Finding Your Path*

**Giving back by paying it forward:** This lesson is linked to gratitude. You have heard the old adage "To those whom much is given, much is expected." I like to believe that the more I give and the more I clean out my closets, the more room I make to receive new gifts. Giving freely without expectation allows you to experience the joy of receiving in a holistic way.

**Choose your friends wisely:** Know the difference between friends and acquaintances. You may have many acquaintances, but only a few friends. True friends want the best for you and behave in a manner that demonstrates their good wishes. Cherish those friends. Most importantly, be your own best friend.

**Forgive: Dump regrets!** Whatever happened to you or by you is possibly over and done with. Forgive others and forgive yourself. Accept your mistakes, make amends and keep moving forward. I understand that forgiveness is not easy, but when it is achieved wholly, both people win. Holding onto bitterness or anger only hardens your heart and is like drinking poison while expecting the other person to die. It just won't happen.

**Accept change:** Don't just accept it, **EMBRACE** change. Whenever there is something you don't like or feel good about, know that change is possible. You can change the situation or you can alter how you feel about it. Either way, change is the answer. Change is the one thing that never sits still, it's always in motion—changing. As you seek to make changes, remember the 10 little two-letter words, "If it is to be, it is up to me." Ten little words that can transform your life.

**Romantic love starts with self-love:** Loving yourself is the basis for this entire book, and especially for the romantic love that most seek. Determine what you want in a love interest. Understand the difference between love and lust. If you so choose, both have a place in your life, but it's important not to confuse one with the other. Remember, forcing a relationship does not work.

**Note the F word, Fear—False Evidence Appearing Real:** We all have a safety zone that we stand in.

Take a chance—come out of there, do something novel or different. Your self-worth is not determined by your success or failure at any endeavor, so go ahead and take a chance. Be clear about what you can or cannot control. The Serenity Prayer offers powerful guidance: "God grant me the serenity to accept the things I cannot change, the courage to change the things I can, and the wisdom to know the difference."

**Look for humor:** This, too, is linked to gratitude. Life is full of humorous situations. Be observant. Sometimes the humor is paired with pathos, making it difficult to discern the bitter from the sweet. Having to go to the bathroom while fleeing the airport terminal during the 9/11 tragedy is both funny and stressful. Humor is one of God's gifts and helps us to be grateful for our situations. Humor, like beauty, is where you find it and in the eye of the beholder.

# 20

## Here's To Life

I have lived a good and full life. Although I have made some mistakes, I have no regrets. Life is not about stumbling and falling down, but rising to the occasion again and again.

There is very little I would change in my past. Obviously, the kidnapping and shooting, my abusive childhood and turbulent romances are experiences I certainly could have lived without.

I have learned that what evil meant for harm, God turned around for good. All the pain of those events provided me with something exceedingly valuable. The ability to live my life on purpose, without fear is priceless. I realize that I am needed. Before the shooting, I would never ask for help. I now ask more freely. I say I love you more, and I really mean those words. I slow down and cherish each day and enjoy every moment.

Through my darkest days and brightest moments,

I have turned to Him and rested on His unwavering strength. I am a blessed child. I am highly favored!

What I know for sure is, I would not have made it without support from others. There have been mentors who have enriched my life. People like my fifth-grade teacher, Mrs. Robinson, who guided me down the right path. Sen. Cecil Partee, former president of the Illinois State Senate, who introduced me to the world of politics.

Chicago Mayor Richard J. Daley was the first one who suggested that I had what it took to run for political office. However, politics was not for me. My grandfather always advised against going into politics because of the dishonesty often associated with politicians. However, he emphasized that we all had a civic obligation to participate in the governmental process and vote. "You should never do anything that would make you give up your right to vote," he said.

Leonard Chess of Chess Records mentored me in radio. Chess owned several radio stations and felt that I was a natural talent and moved me from one station to another. At one time, I had three daily shows on three different stations including WJPC owned by John H. Johnson, the founder of the Johnson Publishing empire.

What I have cherished most about my long career

are the people I have met. My broadcast career has given me a passport to see the world, to witness history in the making.

I met a young community organizer named Barack Obama as he was urging residents to vote in the Hyde Park neighborhood in Chicago. He told them to get involved in the community, know your alderman, vote and encourage others to vote. If your garbage has not been picked up, you can do something about it. See your alderman. Call City Hall. Get involved.

*Here's To Life*

A few years later, I met him again at an event at the Art Institute of Chicago. He walked over to me and said, "I know who you are. I want you to know who I am. I am Barack Obama and I am running for the Illinois Senate."

Even then, he had that remarkable ability to connect with people. His sincerity and commitment to a better America was evident, years before he was overwhelmingly elected as President of the United States of America.

Our paths crossed again when he was the grand marshal of the Bud Billiken Parade in Chicago's Washington Park, one of the biggest parades in the nation. I was the assistant grand marshal and had served as TV host of the nationally televised parade for 23 years.

He and I chatted and took a photo together. I included that photo in this book. It proves how life can turn full circle. I recall riding my shiny new red tricycle through Washington Park when I was 3. Now here I am photographed six decades later, in the same South Side park, talking to a gentleman who would go on to become the 44th President of these United States of America. An African-American man. Wow! Who knew?

Today, I am enjoying my life after my long broadcast career. Retirement is a good thing. It works well for me. My friends say, "it looks good on you." There are weeks when I look at my busy schedule and I ask myself, "Did you really retire?" I guess only from work, not from life.

I am honored to serve as AARP Illinois State President. I accepted the position because I recognized that AARP is the most powerful organization in the country for seniors. In the past, I served organizations that assisted women and children. When I retired from WGN-TV, I faced issues that affect all senior citizens, like choosing health insurance, signing up for Medicare and researching Social Security benefits. I wanted to know my rights as a retiree. AARP speaks to my heart—seasoned as it is.

I find it a privilege to trade wisdom and insight

with others who are growing better with time. Retirement is not the end of work, but the continuation of life. Thanks to medical advances, better nutrition and fitness, we are living longer to enjoy this freedom of time. I urge aging Americans to keep participating in this world. Exercise your body and your mind. Share your knowledge with those less fortunate. Volunteer to teach young children to read. Keep enjoying the everyday miracles.

I am also honored to serve as Commissioner on the Illinois Human Rights Commission. I was honored to be appointed by Governor Pat Quinn and approved by the Illinois Senate. The commission reviews cases that have been through the court system but have been disputed. It gives me unique insight on the tremendous privilege and power of voting in America.

My life is as full as it was before, and even more fulfilling, especially since I now have more time for family and friendships. Last summer I arranged for all of my siblings, who range in age from 83 to 90, to gather in Chicago to vacation for a week with me in a luxurious Lake Geneva home on the lake. They traveled by air and limo, a special indulgence I lavished on them. I have always shared with my family. They are my rock and anything I can do to make them smile and laugh, I have always done and am always ready to do.

*Here's To Life*

We had a marvelous time at the Lake. We were able to spend time reminiscing, laughing and outdoing one another with stories of the past. It was heavenly.

As I am writing this chapter, I learned that my beloved oldest brother, Buster, died at age 88 in Atlanta. My heart is broken. My soul is empty. We are now without our beloved Buster, a proud World War II Army veteran. So many precious memories are rushing through me right now. Life moves so quickly. I have said it over and over again in this book that you must live each day to the fullest. Thank God for every morning because we don't know about tomorrow. Cherish the people around you. I say thank you for each and every moment spent with my family. All we really have in this world is our family.

As I prepared to retire from my broadcast career, a good friend asked what would my legacy be? We typically think of legacies as grand events written in large letters across the pages of history. Truth be told, I always thought I had slacked off in that area. I never entered a flame-engulfed building to rescue trapped children or created a life-saving vaccine.

I did help place thousands of children in loving homes through my work with adoption and foster care. That's a legacy. I raised millions of dollars to send generations of young people to college through the UNCF. That's a legacy that makes me very proud.

Legacies are often simple treasures we leave our families, friends and community. It could be your cherished peach cobbler recipe, the honesty and integrity that you instilled in your children or encouraging words of wisdom.

My daughter is my most prized legacy. She has become such a loving and giving human being and a terrific parent. My love for her and my grandchildren is immeasurable and I pray that my love for them will live on in their hearts forever.

This memoir represents part of my legacy. I have learned that success is not a destination but a journey. I trust that my stumbles and triumphs will guide you on your journey to fulfillment. You too can beat the odds and live a productive and rewarding life.

Take my dad's simple advice: "If it is to be, it is up to me."

## THE END

*Here's To Life*

## LIFE TO LEGACY

Let us bring your story to life! With Life to Legacy, we offer the following publishing services: manuscript development, editing, transcription services, ghostwriting, cover design, copyright services, ISBN assignment, worldwide distribution, and eBooks.

Throughout the entire production process, you maintain control over your project because we are here to serve you. Even if you have no manuscript at all, we can ghostwrite your story for you from audio recordings or legible handwritten documents.

We also specialize in family history books, so you can leave a written legacy for your children, grandchildren and others. You put your story in our hands, and we'll bring it to literary life!

Please visit our website:

www.Life2Legacy.com
or call us at
877-267-7477
You can also e-mail us at:
Life2Legacybooks@att.net